T0150395

REPUBLIC
OF
HINDUTVA

ADVANCE PRAISE FOR THE BOOK

'Given the centrality of the RSS to Indian politics, if not the role it has played over the past seven decades, the paucity of Indian scholars' research on the organization is disappointing. Much of what we read and cite comes from foreign scholars. Noted social scientist Badri Narayan's *Republic of Hindutva* fills this gap. It bristles with great insights, including how the RSS has tried to absorb all social groups, reinterpreted Ambedkar and evolved a strategy of mobilization minus communal riots. It will be essential reading and reference for scholars, journalists and politicians'—Shekhar Gupta, founder and editor-in-chief, ThePrint

'With the help of painstaking fieldwork in Uttar Pradesh and Bihar, Badri Narayan provides a ringside view of the objectives and strategies of the continuously evolving Sangh Parivar. He shows that it is perhaps the only force in India today which understands that building a comprehensive collective narrative is crucial as a means not just for acquiring state power but for retaining it. This short but incisive book is indispensable to anyone keen on understanding the political appeal of Hindutva'—Rajeev Bhargava, honorary fellow and director, Institute of Indian Thought, Centre for the Study of Developing Societies, Delhi

REPUBLIC

OF

HINDUTVA

How the Sangh Is Reshaping Indian Democracy

BADRI NARAYAN

PENGUIN
VIKING

An imprint of Penguin Random House

VIKING

USA | Canada | UK | Ireland | Australia
New Zealand | India | South Africa | China

Viking is part of the Penguin Random House group of companies
whose addresses can be found at global.penguinrandomhouse.com

Published by Penguin Random House India Pvt. Ltd
7th Floor, Infinity Tower C, DLF Cyber City,
Gurgaon 122 002, Haryana, India

First published in Viking by Penguin Random House India 2021

Copyright © Badri Narayan 2021

10 9 8 7 6 5 4 3 2 1

The views and opinions expressed in this book are the author's
own and the facts are as reported by him which have been verified
to the extent possible, and the publishers are not in any way
liable for the same.

ISBN 9780670094042

Typeset in Bembo Std by Manipal Technologies Limited, Manipal
Printed at Thomson Press India Ltd, New Delhi

www.penguin.co.in

To Babuji

'I don't write a book so that it will be the final word; I write a book so that other books are possible, not necessarily written by me.'

—Michel Foucault

CONTENTS

INTRODUCTION

As political analysts all over the world would agree, the stunning rise of the Bharatiya Janata Party (BJP; Indian People's Party) happened due to the political strategies of the current prime minister of India, Narendra Modi, his right-hand man, Amit Shah, who is the current minister of home affairs and a former president of the BJP, as well as the hard work and support of the Rashtriya Swayamsevak Sangh (RSS; National Volunteers Association) and other allied organizations like the Vishwa Hindu Parishad (VHP; Universal Hindu Council) and Bajrang Dal. These comprise the cultural wing of the group known as the Sangh Parivar (Sangh Family), of which the BJP is also a member. Among all the members of the Sangh family, the RSS is the *garbhgriha* (womb) of Hindutva politics. The RSS and the BJP share a very strong bond and the Sangh has contributed a lot in the making and strengthening of the BJP ever since the party was recast in its present form in 1980. The BJP traces its roots to the Bharatiya Jana Sangh (Indian People's Association), which was established in 1951 as the political wing of the RSS by Syama Prasad Mookerjee. Although sometimes the BJP appears as the political wing or mass organization of the RSS, in reality the BJP has developed its own way of creating a hegemonic influence on the Indian public, while the RSS provides organizational support to various BJP political campaigns through its well-organized cadre base.

In the first tenure of Narendra Modi's prime ministership from 2014 to 2019, the RSS had managed to establish itself as an important centre of influence. But what are the dynamics of the relationship between Modi and the RSS? Some analysts believe that although the RSS played an important role in ensuring Modi's victory in the Lok Sabha elections, he is not under pressure to follow the diktats of the RSS regarding political strategies. These analysts don't tire of saying that Modi made the RSS totally ineffective in Gujarat. Another set of analysts believes that the RSS is giving unconditional organizational support to the BJP only to boost Modi's popularity, particularly at the grassroots level. I am of the same opinion. In the Lok Sabha elections, the RSS cadres worked shoulder to shoulder with the BJP's *prachar* (advocacy) team. They toiled at the booth level and provided the campaign strategists with regular feedback from the ground. Thus, a section of the RSS cadres came out of their close-knit *shakha*s (daily training assemblies; literally, 'branches') and entered the rough and tumble of elections. It must also be remembered that Modi was himself an RSS *pracharak* (cadre) for many years before he entered politics. His psyche and world view was formed and nurtured by the Sangh. Of course, during his tenure as the Gujarat chief minister he moved beyond the RSS mould and came to be known as a business-friendly, tech-savvy administrator.

In this book, I will try to tell the story of democracy and elections that unfolded in India in 2014 and 2019 from the perspective of Hindutva politics. It is based on extensive fieldwork, over several years, in different parts of India, especially in Uttar Pradesh (UP) and Bihar, which I undertook to understand the rise and growth of Hindutva. I will discuss how the forms and processes of Hindutva politics deal with the politics of democracy in India.

My attempt is to document how organizations based on the Hindutva ideology, such as the RSS and its affiliates, work at the grassroots to ensure their expansion socially, culturally and politically. I will also question the stereotypes and myths about Hindutva politics, organizations and their sociopolitical actions, which exist due to certain biases resulting from our distance from grassroot realities. It is interesting to observe how ideology translates into practice at the grassroots and how those experiences and insights bring changes in turn in the structure of Hindutva-influenced organizations. It is also interesting to see how through their grassroots initiatives, Hindutva forces are reshaping Indian democracy in their own ways.

The RSS as an organization is both a reality and a myth. There can be no final word on it. One of the reasons for this is that it is continuously changing and evolving. It constantly destroys and renews its image. As mentioned, the Sangh has many allied organizations such as the BJP, VHP and the Bajrang Dal, which together constitute the Sangh Parivar. But what isn't known is that there are many small social, cultural and educational outfits that aren't allies of the Sangh but are closely associated with the RSS. These are outfits like Rashtriya Sewa Bharti, Vidya Bharti, Vandemataram, Vanvasi Kalyan Ashram, Keshav Sharanam, Shiksha Sanskriti Utthan Nyas, Shishu Shiksha Prabandh Samiti, Sahakar Bharati (a microfinance unit of Sangh Parivar), which are active in many states and are used to spread the RSS message. Many other small organizations working on different social projects active in various parts of India are named after Hindu gods and goddesses in order to make them more attractive to Hindus. However, it should be mentioned that these organizations function independently of the RSS. For example, the Saraswati Shishu Mandir schools that have branches in several parts of UP are not run by the RSS but the RSS message is imparted to the students in these schools. Several schools and intermediate colleges in cities like Prayagraj (earlier known as Allahabad), Kanpur, Lucknow and Varanasi are heavily influenced by the RSS. These institutions are run by people involved with the RSS and many teachers are members of the RSS. They regularly organize activities targeting different sections and age groups, including workshops for children, *katha mandals* (religious and spiritual discourses) and *keertan mandals* (religious chants and songs) for women and senior citizens. The aim is simple: creating a Hindu consciousness and spreading the message of Hindutva. Some of these events are on such a large scale that even the top RSS leaders like Mohan Bhagwat, the *sarsanghchalak* (chief) of the RSS, attend them.

While conducting fieldwork on the RSS, this unofficial and unclaimed part of the RSS left us awestruck. We realized that the RSS is like the tip of an iceberg. The part which is invisible is much larger than the part which is visible. Political analysts who hold forth on the RSS in heated television debates do not understand the real power of the RSS. They use relatively superficial aspects like electoral successes and communalism to define the RSS. The problem of the Opposition is that they are fighting with an image of the RSS which is not its reality. The RSS is changing day by day but the politicians of the opposition parties are attacking the image of the RSS which is much older and has become obsolete. The political forces attacking the RSS are in fact attacking its shadow but are unable to understand the real RSS.

Sometimes the RSS's activities suit Modi's agenda. But the RSS is also developing a new politics of Hindutva, a process that is independent of the prime minister. Of course, Modi's rise has been helpful to the RSS. Modi and the RSS are thus complementary to each other in this sense.

The RSS has always been an object of scrutiny in Indian political discourse, but not enough effort has been made to understand it intellectually. There have been a number of notable attempts. Among the two books by Walter K. Andersen and Sridhar K. Damle, *RSS: A View to the Inside* offers an overview of the history of the RSS, its ideas and ideology, some changes over the years, the people who made it and who changed it. It also includes the rise of Narendra Modi as prime minister. Its prequel, *The Brotherhood in Saffron: The Rashtriya Swayamsevak Sangh and Hindu Revivalism*, gives a glimpse into the inner workings of the RSS. Des Raj Goyal's book, *Rashtriya Swayamsewak Sangh*, also talks about the ideology, culture and politics of the RSS, and its role in the overall right-wing ecosystem in India. Dhirendra K. Jha's *Shadow Armies: Fringe Organizations and Foot Soldiers of Hindutva* talks about the numerous overt and covert organizations affiliated to the RSS. Sunil Ambekar, himself an insider of the RSS, in his insightful book, *The RSS: Roadmaps for the 21st Century*, tries to answer many questions about the RSS that have puzzled intellectuals and the general public alike. While some of these books make an effort to understand the emergence of a new kind of the RSS and learn about their new issues, agendas and ways of mobilization, most of the existing body of literature, including booklets, looks at the Sangh through an activist lens or a partisan position.

A new RSS, which includes elements of the old RSS, can be seen emerging in the current scenario in our country. The changes are visible in the Sangh's outlook and activities, where it has adapted to a modern idiom and logic generated by democratic values. This change has occurred across the several affiliated organizations that are active on the ground. The cadres of this new RSS are not shy in participating in politics at the grassroots level and are working at various levels—from booth management to input-giving agency. Additionally, they are also working to resolve the discontent among the leaders of the BJP that often appears during the time of elections. The present RSS has developed a skill to appropriate communities usually considered non-Hindutva political material, such as Dalits, tribals and other marginalized communities. The large Dalit community in north India is a major target group for the RSS now since all the major political parties of India are competing to get their votes. The BJP's success in garnering Dalit votes in both the 2014 and 2019 Lok Sabha elections was the result of a long process of mobilization by the RSS at the grassroots level.

The mission of the RSS now is to create a cultural hegemony that will include the entire Hindu community and even many traditionally non-Hindu tribals and other minority groups.[1] Now, Hindutva organizations are involved in creating a Hindutva narrative on social sites or in training their cadre for mobilizing as many

social groups as possible into their fold.[2]
I attempt to show in this book that during both
the parliamentary and Assembly elections in
the last few years, the BJP and the RSS have
focused on the fact that UP is a highly caste-
divided state and winning elections there
depends more on the number of castes a party
is able to enfold with the promises of roads,
hospitals and schools. This contradicts the
claims of some political analysts that the BJP's
victory proves the erasure of caste from Indian
electoral politics.[3] It is a victory achieved by the
mobilization of the various desires expressed
by different communities, such as for caste
identity, Hindutva aspiration and development.

One commonly held belief about the RSS
is that all its volunteers are old, orthodox and
out of sync with today's world. This couldn't
be farther from the truth. The RSS volunteers
have become increasingly technology-savvy.
They have taken to social media in a big way
and use the latest mediums to spread their
message. Every volunteer who joins the RSS
is given a diary in which the phone numbers

of all the members are listed. According to a high-ranking RSS leader, new technology and new means of transport haven't weakened the Sangh; rather, its way of functioning has become smoother. Thus, in order to understand the RSS, we have to see how it has adapted to the times and reinvented itself. The RSS is not only an organization but also works as a coordinating organization for many organizations that work on its sociocultural and political lines.

We need to also understand how the RSS works as an organization that cultivates a Hindutva mind and consciousness, which helps to politically mobilize the electorate for supporting the BJP. We may also find a balance of synergies between the RSS and the BJP, which may give an impressive political result in favour of the BJP. One cannot deny that there may be differences of opinion on various issues between the many affiliates of the Sangh Parivar, but the RSS has successfully created a synthesis among all these contradictory opinions that emerge from time to time between its affiliates, leaders and cadres. This book is a documentation of the political aspect of the Hindutva Parivar and the political actions that emerge during democratic elections in India.

The book is divided into six chapters. The first chapter, 'Reinventing the RSS: Perception and Reality', is an overview of the RSS with a short description about its functioning. We will discuss how the new RSS derives its strength from the invented tradition of Indian society and is preparing the socialcultural context for the strengthening of the BJP. We will also discuss how the RSS is trying to identify the most marginal castes in different parts of the country and then trying to tap into their unfulfilled desires.

In the second chapter, 'Appropriation as Process: Caste, Dalits and Hindutva', we will discuss how through tactics of appropriation and accommodation the RSS is co-opting social groups like Dalits, tribals and minorities, and how as a proponent of Hindutva-based politics the RSS with its Hindutva Parivar, is handling caste in its mobilizational campaigns. In the third chapter, 'Forging a New Mobilizational Consciousness', we will discuss the changing forms of polarization politics and what it means for democratic electoral politics in India. It was earlier assumed that the communal politics in which the BJP and the RSS indulged led to communal riots in several parts of the country. In this chapter I will show, through my work on the ground and conducting interviews and interactions with the RSS cadres and pracharaks active in UP over several years, that the new RSS, in a break from its old radical image, does not want to create communal tensions in society.

In chapter 4, 'The RSS in Elections: Political and Apolitical', I will describe how RSS cadres not only generate discourses and symbolic resources that help the BJP disseminate its influence but also informally help the BJP in organizing election campaigns. We will try to understand the role of the RSS in the election campaign of the present prime minister of India, Narendra Modi, in the 2014 parliamentary elections, particularly in the making and building of his image as the prime ministerial candidate.

In chapter 5, 'Politics, Narratives and Elections', we will see how the BJP and the Hindutva family formed their narrative during democratic elections especially in UP, and how other parties explored their resource base for their own narratives. In this chapter we have evolved our discourses based on the context of the parliamentary elections in 2014 and 2019, and the 2017 UP state Assembly election. In chapter 6, 'The Road Ahead: Framing Own Public', we will analyse what are the challenges before the Sangh and its affiliates and how they are going to resolve them. We will also analyse how the Narendra Modi–led government is going to influence various groups and what new elements he and his government will add to the politics of democracy in India.

We conclude the book by mapping the new and unconventional relationships between democracy and Hindutva groups in Indian politics.

As an epilogue to these changes and shifts taking place in Indian democracy and society, we touch upon the impact of the outbreak of the novel coronavirus COVID-19 in the year 2020. A new kind of public, the 'bio-public', was in the process of being formed, which gave primacy to biological safety over all social considerations, hitherto considered entrenched in Indian society. We examine how this may affect the Sangh Parivar's programme of creating a Hindutva public. When normalcy is restored, would they be able to use the social work they have done during this emergency time to create an easy transition from the 'bio-public' to the Hindutva public? Only time can tell.

1

REINVENTING THE RSS

Perception and Reality

Shakti ki karo maulik kalpana, karo pujan
Chhor do samar, jab tak na siddhi ho, Raghunandan

—Suryakant Tripathi Nirala[1]

(Perceive Shakti for yourself, worship her
Till you realize her,
Take a break from war, O Raghunandan)

My first introduction to the RSS was when I was studying in class eight in a school in Arrah, Bihar. I started participating in the shakha that was held in Veer Kunwar Singh Park in Arrah town. Attending the shakha daily and participating in almost all the Hindu festivals organized in the RSS office in Karman Tola became part of my everyday life. However, at around the same time, I also became associated with the leftist writers' groups active in those days in the same town, and consequently began to see the RSS through a leftist lens. Through popular left-wing booklets and the discourses of leftist leaders, a stereotypical image of the RSS emerged in my mind in the 1980s. This led to a dwindling of my association with the organization, gradually ending it altogether after some years. I spent more than thirty years of my life with that Left-invented image of the RSS.

Once, an eminent social science scholar told me that had he been in my place, he may have joined the RSS and tried to write a good book on it based on inside information. It was difficult for me to resume my ties with the RSS with all the intellectual baggage that I carried, so I decided to work on a long-term project to understand it from the outside. As a part of this effort I began to document their presence in Indian society and politics. From my observations during my fieldwork in the last thirty years in various parts of UP, I gradually understood that the RSS that I was seeing in the field was not the same RSS that had been there in my perception in the decades of the 1980s and '90s. In these intervening three or four decades, Indian society and politics had undergone tremendous changes, which had also influenced the RSS, leading to the emergence of its new form with new ideas.

However, my friends active in the RSS seem uncomfortable with this concept of a new RSS. They see the present RSS as a continuum of its original form and content. They refuse to accept that there is any change in it. But we all have observed in the past few years a new form of the RSS which is vibrantly interacting with the media, using social media actively, debating about its ideology with its opponents, and doing social service as the biggest NGO (non-governmental organization) of the country. This is an RSS which is gradually increasing its appetite to swallow all the social groups that have been opposed to its sociocultural politics.

On the ground, a new RSS is emerging, but our approaches to understand it are unfortunately still old. The RSS today has not only imbibed many elements from its old avatar but has also added new elements to its character and structure. This transformation manifests not only in switching from khaki half pants to brown pants, but is also seen in the new Sangh's outlook and activities. The RSS has also assimilated within it the new logic and arguments produced by democracy and modernity alongside traditional Hindu and religious language. For instance, it is talking about social issues related to gender, ecology, development and now the COVID-19 pandemic. The introduction of modern content in its traditional language has changed the texture of the latter. The form of this new Sangh emerges not only in a single organization but is shaped by thousands of affiliated organizations which are active in society in their own way and are influencing various social groups. We are aware of organizations like Vidya Bharti and its Saraswati Shishu

Mandir schools, but we may not know that under the RSS's banner almost 800 NGOs are actively working nationwide in various sectors, including providing disaster relief during emergencies and natural calamities and eradicating poverty.

As is inevitable, ideological conflicts and discussions occur among the Sangh and its affiliates. For instance, organizations such as the Bharatiya Mazdoor Sangh (Indian Workers' Union) and the Swadeshi Jagran Manch (Indigenous Awakening Forum) have contrasting viewpoints from the BJP and the RSS on various issues, and have been protesting against the Central government's policies on land acquisition and liberalization respectively.[2] By summoning the ideological contestations produced by its affiliated organizations on different social and class issues, the Sangh is attempting to frame a holistic argument. A number of communities exist in Indian society at different levels of awareness regarding their needs, so it is understandable that contradictions will emerge from these groups. This is also known as 'developmental consciousness' about the quality of life, about the basic needs and requirements, which varies among the different classes. This will also reflect in the political and cultural organizations representing these groups. The Sangh has made the space for these contradictions in its discussions and debates by creating a relationship with its affiliated organizations akin to that of a body with its parts.

Bowing to democratic imperatives—such as equality and justice in a broad sense—and the pressure of international and diasporic social groups, the outlook of the RSS on several topical issues like homosexuality or transgender people has also changed. Largely, it no longer openly supports the 'traditional' viewpoint on these issues, and does not consider it to be a crime for someone to be in a gay or lesbian relationship.[3] In tune with the times, the Sangh also proposes to support the reservation policy for socially oppressed communities. Earlier, the participation of women in Sangh activities was almost negligible but now emphasis is being laid on it. The Rashtriya Sevika Samiti (the women's wing of the RSS) is continuously organizing leadership development programmes for its members with a focus on *matritva* (universal motherhood), *kratritva* (efficiency and social activism) and *netritva* (leadership).

As a part of its strategy to bring more and more sections of the population under its wing, the RSS is constantly trying to reach the social communities who are not yet under its influence. Dalits, tribals and Muslims are the groups on which the RSS is working hard. The big change we have witnessed in recent years is the RSS's outreach to Dalits through its *samajik samrasta* (social harmony) campaign as well as a more accommodative stance towards Dr B.R. Ambedkar. An early indication of this change in outlook towards the Dalit icon came in a book written by Sangh ideologue Krishna Gopal (with Shri Prakash) in 2014, called *Rashtra-Purush Baba Saheb Dr. Bhimrao Ambedkar*. In it, he projects Ambedkar as the greatest icon of samajik samrasta, and that everyone should follow his shown path to provide social dignity to the deprived. It can be asserted that the BJP's effort to associate itself with Ambedkar is the political outcome of the Sangh's new appraisal of him.

Ambedkar was seen as a strong critic of the Hindu caste system by the radical Ambedkarite movement in India. He had once said that he was born as a Hindu but will not die a Hindu.[4] He was of the view that there is no escape from one's birth-based caste location within Hinduism. Thus, he chose to convert to Buddhism in 1956, just a few months before his death. Inspired by him, a large section of Dalits also converted to Buddhism. One can observe the trend of adopting Buddhism among a section of newly educated higher and middle-class north-Indian Dalits. But during our fieldwork in the villages of UP and Bihar, we also observed that their conversion in terms of religious memories from Hinduism to Buddhism is not yet fully complete. Some of them still live with the memories of their Hindu beliefs and lifestyle, while their identity is Buddhist. They are still not able to stop themselves from celebrating some Hindu festivals and worshipping some Hindu deities along with revering Buddha and Ambedkar. During the wedding ceremonies of some of the neo-Buddhist families in the Hindi-speaking regions,[5] the worship of Ganesha and Buddha takes place together, and the icons can be seen next to each other on several wedding invitation cards. The case of Maharashtra may be different, but in many Hindi-speaking regions this phenomenon is common.

The Hindutva movement, as led by the Sangh, is trying to convert Ambedkar into a relatable symbol for everyone by downplaying his critique of the caste system. They want to detach his persona that critiqued the caste system from the version of him that they have invented. Their strategies are twofold. The first is if all Hindus across castes start respecting Ambedkar, his critique of the Hindu religion can be sidelined from the memories of Dalits and other oppressed communities. Secondly, they are constantly trying to rebuild Ambedkar's image based on a selective forgetting of his critique. His image is used as a brand icon for the samrasta campaign, as a part of the drive to assimilate Dalits into the Hindu fold. In order to attach the elements of divinity, rituals and worship to the image of Ambedkar, it is expedient for Hindutva forces to associate themselves with the symbolic power that lies within it. There are calendars and portraits of Ambedkar in many RSS offices. In their public programmes too the portrait of Ambedkar occupies centre stage. The BJP government also took various steps to prove that they pay more respect to Ambedkar's memories, symbols and memorials than done by the Congress government during its rule. For instance, it turned five places in Delhi, Mumbai, Nagpur, Mhow and London connected with Ambedkar into pilgrimage spots. The government of Maharashtra purchased Ambedkar's house in 2015 in order to create a memorial museum to him. Modi inaugurated the memorial on 14 November 2015. He had earlier laid the foundation stone for the Dr Ambedkar International Centre in Delhi on 20 April 2015.[6]

In addition, the Sangh is constantly responding to changes in the Indian socio-economic landscape ushered in by economic liberalization and to the new technologically constructed public sphere. As it forges its relationship with modernity, democracy, the market and new technology, and evolves under their influence, it is using all the fruits of modernity in its functioning. With smartphones, social media sites and online media, the RSS is working creatively and channelling traditional resources of Indian society for its new mobilizational politics.

Orality and Mobilization

This new RSS is reinterpreting Indian history and culture, giving new meaning to traditional discourses that suits its contemporary ideological requirements. I find that much of the BJP's popularity today has to do with the sociocultural mindset that the Sangh has formed in the last fifty to sixty years through its groundwork. The Sangh has slowly, without worrying about media attention, formed a large group of dedicated and able workers, who are active from the top to the lowest levels, be it for elections or opinion-making, group mobilization or sociocultural activities. Through its training camps (*varga*), the Sangh is, it claims, preparing over a lakh cadre every year.[7]

During my research I observed that the greatest strength of the Sangh is its language of mobilization. Understanding this strength, a Congress leader says, 'In the language of the Sangh, one hears the echo of 5000 years. It has internalized many of Indian traditions. If the Congress has to strengthen [its position vis-à-vis the BJP], it must develop a counter language loaded with the image of past, present and future of Indian society.' The Sangh uses language that reflects the sixteen stages of life as in Hinduism (*samskaras*), which defines a person's life from birth to death. If you closely analyse the *bauddhiki* (speech delivered by the

RSS pracharaks) at the vargas, you can discern the source of this language, the strategy of its construction and its form.

There is an impressive storytelling element in the speeches of the volunteers, which is the regular culture of their shakhas and vargas. Through these stories the struggle, motivation and aim of the Sangh are narrated. An important element in all the speeches of the Sangh is the element of valour. Poems composed by Ramdhari Singh Dinkar and other nationalist poets, who have used this element, are recited.[8] The storytelling style of the volunteers reminds us of the Indian storytelling tradition in which the ancient mythological texts like the *Bhagvad Purana*, the Mahabharata, *Satyanarayan Vrat Katha*, etc., are narrated and heard widely. In the same narrative technique, workers of the Sangh develop their lectures with new content. We know that tales and stories are deeply rooted in the Indian psyche. For instance, people in villages often use tales and idioms to communicate their message. Our society's childlike imagination weaves its dreams by hearing tales along with religious and moral narratives. Perhaps understanding this mindset, the poems that are used in the discourse of the Sangh have tales, both modern and old. Images and characters emerge and are used to motivate people. The audience becomes enthralled by these speeches; it is because of the hypnotic effect of these tales that M.S. Golwalkar, the second sarsanghchalak of the RSS, imagined the following structure of an Indian village, inspired by the suggestion of Madan Mohan Malaviya: '*sabha*s [assemblies] in every village, tales in every *sabha*, schools in every village, along with *mallashala* [wrestling grounds]'. In one of Malaviya's slokas composed in Sanskrit he had opined:

> *Grame-grame sabhakarya, grame grame katha shubha*
> *Pathshala, mallshala pratiparv mahotsavah*

In every village there should be an assembly from where villagers may get religious teachings and practical suggestions. In every

village there should be storytelling based
on our ancient traditions. There should be
a school and a wrestling ground in every
village.[9]

Another strategy of these discourses is the
attempt to assimilate, in which the Sangh
is trying to co-opt different and opposing
ideologies in it. Through these efforts, the
criticism of Hindu religion by Ambedkar and
neo-Buddhists disappears and an interactive
relation between Hinduism and Buddhism
emerges. Alongside, in the recent past, Dalit
groups have identified with many minor
characters in Hindu texts and presented them
as symbols of injustice done to them. Efforts are
being made to highlight such minor characters
within the discourses of the Sangh, in which they
and their identities could be given respect. For
instance, they project the character of Eklavya
from the Mahabharata as a *dharmaparayan*
Dalit (a Dalit who follows his dharma), who
sacrificed his thumb in reverence to his guru.
In the process, they underplay the aspect of

injustice by Dronacharya, which Ambedkarite Dalits highlight. Using the Eklavya myth in this way, they claim the Dalit community has traditionally produced Dharmaparayan Dalit Mahapurush (great dharma-following Dalit men) and that as a community Dalits are totally committed to Hindu cultural values.

Under this strategy some initiatives have also been undertaken to evolve a larger narrative with different kinds of meanings and relations developed from characters, tales and religions that previously stood against or in opposition to them. Take, for instance, the construction of the Shabari temple; a different depiction of the relationship between Ram, Hanuman and the forest dwellers; and initiating temple construction along with school and cleaning projects in tribal villages. In northern India, the Sangh is not unaware of local and little traditions popular among marginal communities. It is constantly trying to explore and assimilate them in its metanarrative (see chapter 2 for more details). This process of assimilation at the level of language is not easy or straightforward, but is full of conflicts and intricacies. Small or micro-narratives often tend to be dissenting in nature and sometimes deconstruct the metanarrative itself. The pracharak tries to tone down the dissonant aspect to make it easy to absorb. This process creates a rupture in the RSS's traditional language, its texture and tone. For instance, when the RSS has to deal with the Dalit identity, it uses two words: 'Dalit' and '*vanchit*' (unprivileged). These two words are not merely terms. A large section of the literate Dalit community identifies itself as Dalit, which connotes a politically empowered community. But when the RSS attempts to bring them under a broader 'vanchit' identity, it generates tension. This transformation of Dalit to vanchit creates processual conflicts. The RSS pracharaks try to synthesize this conflict. Only a few very efficient and senior pracharaks are able to do this successfully.

Here I wish to assert that the discourses of the Sangh are not spontaneous. These narratives emerge under the influence of aims, objectives and contemporary needs of the

Sangh conceptualized by their top leadership. While there is appropriation of smaller and neglected subaltern traditions in the RSS discourse at many places, the greatest challenge of the workers is how to resolve the internal conflicts within the metanarratives. For this, the feedback of the RSS cadres working among various social groups at the grassroots level is very important. Sometimes they manage to resolve them, but sometimes they are not so successful. But their efforts to widen their narrative are constant. For example, the stories of forest dwellers along the North-eastern borders and those of Dalit groups are now slowly entering the narratives of the RSS. It remains to be seen how the Sangh manages to assimilate opposing and conflicting narratives.

Religious Space and Influence

While visiting a village in UP called Kabutara Basti, in Bundelkhand in 2017, we met an activist of the RSS who was holding a meeting of the people of the Kabutara caste. He was urging them to construct a temple of their village deity who was worshipped as a small mound under the neem tree of the village.[10] Kabutara is one of the most marginalized small communities known for making alcohol and selling it in rural areas. The people of this community sell the alcohol in polythene packs at dirt-cheap rates. They face police atrocities every day because their means of livelihood have been declared illegal by the state administration. They told us that they somehow earn a living, but wanted a space where they could convey their suffering to God and also pray for their desires to be fulfilled. In our interview with the RSS cadre, he said that the RSS had done a survey of the villages to identify the most marginal caste and find out their desires. Through this process, they understood that this poor community had a strong, unfulfilled desire to construct a temple for their community deity. We also spoke to a few senior Sangh cadres working in that region. They informed us that they were working among the most marginalized communities, whom they called *ati-vanchit samooh* (very deprived group), such as the Sahariya, Kabutara, Nat (community of dancers, singers and acrobats), Sapera (snake charmer), etc., to provide them a *dharmasthan* (religious place) of their own. Most of the Sapera community in UP are the followers of Nath Panth, a religious sect made popular by a medieval-era saint, Guru Gorakhnath. During our fieldwork in a few villages inhabited by them, we too observed their strong urge to have a temple, in which they wanted to install an idol of Guru Gorakhnath along with the statue of Shiva. The Saperas of these villages also wanted to invite Yogi Adityanath, the mahant of the Nath Panth and currently the chief minister of UP, if they succeeded in building the temple.

Bundelkhand is an underdeveloped region of UP which consists of four parliamentary constituencies. Bundeli is the local dialect spoken in this region. The terrain is difficult, with forests, hill tracts and riverine areas. Bundelkhand suffers from high outbound migration and displacement due to poverty and unavailability of livelihood. There is paucity of drinking water in addition to lack of water resources to irrigate lands, which affects agricultural production. There are two types of migration taking place from this land: male migration and migration of entire families. The deserted family of the male migrant is a social reality in this region. This is the land of growing rural distress and has witnessed many peasant and farmer suicides. Many marginalized communities live here, including those within the Most Backward Castes (MBCs) and Schedules Castes (SCs). The MBCs, not part of the SC bracket, are an extremely deprived and less visible community; although they are not 'untouchable', they fall in the lowest rung of the caste hierarchy among the backward castes.[11] This area is also inhabited by semi-nomadic communities, tribal communities and most marginalized SC communities.[12]

The Sahariya community is one of the most backward and marginalized communities of all in this region. On a visit to one of their localities near Lalitpur, we heard a vocal demand from them to make a temple for their local deity, along with other demands like secure jobs, pension, and so on. They thought we were political leaders and had come to appeal for votes. For them elections provided an opportunity to present their demands to the political leaders, of whichever party. The neta does not mean the person who is contesting Lok Sabha polls. It means the person who has come to appeal for votes. By talking to the local leaders, they think that they have expressed their needs before the *sarkar* (government). Sometimes the *gram pradhan* (village chief) also appears as a representative of the sarkar to them.

The Nats are another semi-nomadic community who are settled in some parts of Bundelkhand. They have their own traditional deity installed under the peepul tree where they worship with rice and vermilion. However, they desired a temple for their deity in that area. This was their demand during the 2017 UP Assembly election season. Kuchhbadhiya is another small community whose traditional occupation is to make rope from barks of trees and sell it. Some people of this caste whom I interviewed wanted the government to construct a temple in their locality. They felt that since the upper-caste locality had a big Shiva temple with a large space for water, they too wanted a similar temple for their deity.

There are many Dalit communities in UP who have their own gods/goddesses and desire the construction of temples or attribution of religious sites to them. For example, the Dusadh community in Bihar is an important Dalit community and one will find temples of various gods and goddesses close to their settlements, along with temples of Chuharmal, Sahle and Goreya Dev. However, the snake charmer community aspires to construct a temple of Peer Goga, who is considered the god of snakes, but they do not have the socio-economic strength to realize their wish and they plan to demand it during the 2022 Assembly elections.

The deities of these small, marginalized communities are not deities like Ram, Shiva and Hanuman, who are in the larger Hindu pantheon, but local deities like Agaramata and Tonki Devi. These deities are not only their gods but also the identity markers of their community. Their desire for the temples carries not only religious meaning but also a social one. The temple would be a space where they can worship their clan or village deities as well as where they assemble, sit together, sing bhajans and share the joys and sorrows of everyday life. So, for marginalized communities, a temple is not merely a religious or sacred space; it also expresses their desire to acquire a social space that provides them a sense of acceptance, and for gaining respect and dignity. The RSS seems to have grasped this social meaning entangled with religious meaning around the desire for local temples. We discovered that the RSS had conducted a survey in various villages of Bundelkhand and had emerged as a support system for fulfilling such desires of the most marginalized communities.[13] With this, it extended its organizational influence among these poor communities.

The desire for 'identity' and 'development' is the focal point of today's politics and political discourse mobilization. Whenever we talk about the aspiration for identity, we emphasize the social and political identity. We are neither sensitive to nor conscious about the role of religion in the construction of identity in any social group. When political parties build their agenda around the identity of Dalits, tribals and marginalized groups, or make an attempt to understand it, they don't pay much attention to the religious feelings of these groups. While researching Dalit and marginalized social groups, we have found that their desire for religious identity is coherently interwoven with their desire for social respect. For them, the meaning of respect is equal participation in religious spaces as well.

This desire for religious space is not a new phenomenon; it has been there since marginalized groups became conscious of the problem of untouchability. Their desire for freedom from untouchability has been closely associated with the desire for food and water, and also for equality within Hinduism. For instance, the Adi Hindu movement of Swami Achhootanand around 1920 was an important effort to provide religious identity to Dalits. Being disillusioned by the Arya Samaj, Achhootanand and his followers formulated the ideology of 'Adi Hindu', a pre-Aryan identity for the Untouchables as the original inhabitants—*adi* Hindus—of India. They stressed the role of education in upward mobility and sociocultural emancipation of Dalits. The Adi Hindus were strong supporters of Ambedkar and led several protests and rallies to support his demand for separate electorates. This movement effectively facilitated the creation of Dalit consciousness. Along with their daily bread, oppressed groups crave a space where they can be equals and experience spiritual relief to confront the struggles of everyday life. They also want to experience a brotherhood based on such equality. It is unfortunate that they do not even find the space to pray to their gods and to cry.

For Marx, religion was the opium of the people, but he had also admitted that religion was the cry of the oppressed heart.[14] If you ever visit the Ravidas fair in Varanasi, you will find many people standing in queues with their eyes full of tears throwing coins and gold at the idol of Ravidas—a fifteenth-century saint, *bhakt* (devotee) and mystic poet. Even the Dalit groups who have gained economic independence desire a religious space and respect. You will find even NRIs (non-resident Indians) eating onion–chapatti along with the local poor people in Ravidas fairs. In addition to the Ravidassia Panth, Kabir Panth and Shivanarayan Panth have emerged as religious spaces where marginalized communities get the space for their plea of pain, and the desire for equality and respect.[15]

Understanding this desire of Dalits, political leaders like Kanshiram and Mayawati worked consciously on the politics of paying respect to their saints and gurus, and to mobilize and organize Dalits around them. The Bahujan Samaj Party (BSP), the political party conceived by Kanshiram, laid a strong emphasis on identity and self-respect by creating icons and symbols based on the culture of Dalits as markers of their pride and glory.[16] Towards this aim, it commemorated saints like Kabir and Ravidas. Among other memorials, it has created the Rashtriya Dalit Prerna Sthal in Noida, the Dr Bhimrao Ambedkar Samajik Parivartan Prateek Sthal (Ambedkar Memorial) and the Bahujan Samaj Prerna Kendra in Lucknow, and Ravidas temples and deras in Punjab. Rural Dalits aspire to have the freedom to worship their ancestral gods/goddesses. Earlier, they tried to fulfil this desire by installing and worshipping small idols on the mud platform below peepul trees. Now they are asserting themselves by constructing small temples in their hamlets.

However, Dalit society feels the need to express itself more freely and openly, and this aspiration is expressed through the desire for their own mandirs as well as, in some instances, for temples of Hindu gods and goddesses. Those who are economically better off desire the freedom to visit religious sites and celebrate religious festivals in public spaces along with the upper castes. In addition, Dalits have reinvented Buddhism as their religious ground. For example, a Dalit priest heads the rituals at Bauddh Vihar in Shravasti. In Prayagraj, an eminent Dalit writer/activist is an advocate and a Buddhist priest (*bhante*). He is secretary general of the Bharatiya Bauddha Parishad (Indian Buddhists Organization), established by Ambedkar. Several NGOs like the Golden Triangle Foundation and the Missionaries of Lord Buddha are active in Prayagraj for marginalized communities.

Dr B.R. Ambedkar had initiated the landmark movement for temple entry for Dalits. Mahatma Gandhi had understood the need and tried to carve respect for Dalits (whom he had named 'Harijan'—Lord Krishna's people) within Hinduism. Another effort was made by the Arya Samaj, as it constructed a religious identity for Dalits and the marginalized, and tried to provide them respect by associating them with Vedic culture. Many other contemporary social movements also advocated movements like temple entry. In the same vein, albeit with a different purpose, RSS leader Tarun Vijay tried to facilitate the entry of a group of Dalits into a temple of Uttarakhand.[17]

While visiting Jayapura, the village near Varanasi in UP that was adopted in November 2014 by Prime Minister Narendra Modi, we saw that there is a separate hamlet of the Musahar community named Atalnagar. At the entrance to this hamlet a small temple had been constructed close to a tree, in which, along with Shiva, the idol of Mata Shabari (the goddess of the Musahar community) had been placed. The Musahar community had wished for a Mata Shabari temple for quite some time, but they neither had the economic capacity nor social strength to construct it. They appeared to be a happy group after the temple's construction. They asserted with pride that there was no other temple of Mata Shabari within a fifty-kilometre radius.[18]

The RSS has understood that community gods are important symbols of assertion for the identity of marginalized communities. It is trying to build up its influence by tapping such issues.

The RSS is also trying to weave the Hindu community together by using the hegemonic influences that lie in the smaller sects like the Nath Panth, the sect of the Bhakti saint Sankardev who is popular in the North-east, especially in Assam, the Kabir Panth, and many locally important religious sects in different parts of India.

With its affiliates like the Vishwa Hindu Parishad (Universal Hindu Council) and Dharm Jagran Samiti (Religious Awakening Committee), the RSS is constantly working to disseminate Hindutva ideology through various public platforms associated with Hinduism, such as Ram Katha Mandal, Bhagwat Katha Mandal, other kirtan mandals, and the those that emerged from the activities of various akharas, Sanatan Dharam groups, *math*s (monasteries) and mandirs, etc. These religious public spheres disseminate the values and morals of Hinduism and also discuss various political and national happenings based on the Hindutva ideological framework. The discourses of these public spheres become influential among their followers due to their inherent faith in Hinduism and trust in Hindu values. Unlike Western public spheres, these Indian public spheres do not work merely through argument and logic, but through faith as well. The Sangh and Hindutva politics are becoming increasingly influential by the day due to their reach into the non-political but socially, culturally and religiously powerful public spheres associated with Hinduism.

In Chhattisgarh, there are several katha mandalis like the Chanchal Manas Mandali, Tonapar Manas Mandali, Sinodha, Shri Ram Manas Mandali, Mali Dih, etc. These are a few examples of the lakhs of Ram Katha Mandals active in different parts of Chhattisgarh. These Ram Katha Mandals are creating very vibrant public forums in various parts of Hindi-dominant states such as Madhya Pradesh (MP), UP, Bihar, Rajsthan, and even reaching non-Hindi-speaking states like Haryana and Orissa. Many Ram Katha *pravachak*s (narrators) and saints and sadhus who recite the Bhagwat Katha attract lakhs of people when they narrate these tales in different parts of India. Some among the popular Ram Katha pravachaks are Murari Bapu, Jagad Guru Ramswaroopa Acharyaji Maharaj, Prem Bhushanji Maharaj, Anuradha Saraswatiji, and among Bhagwat Katha narrators are Devakinandanji Thakurji Maharaj, Devi Priyankaji, Manojji Maharaj (Saharanpur-wale), Pandit Ramji Sharma (Vrindavan-wale). If one were to interact with these storytellers, one may find that most of them are impressed by Hindutva politics in one way or another. During their discourse and storytelling, they also discuss issues like the Ram Janambhoomi temple, Article 370, and issues like 'triple talaq', sometimes as a passing reference. Recently, the chief minister of UP, Yogi Adityanath inaugurated a nine-day-long Ram Katha Utsav by the famous Murari Bapu in Gorakhpur and gave a hint of the 'good news' about the construction of the Ram temple in Ayodhya.[19]

Perception and Politics of Projection

While on the one hand the Sangh is deriving its strength from various sources and evolving a language and discourse which has become popular among large numbers of the rural and urban poor, it is simultaneously being targeted by the parties in the Opposition. But the problem of the Opposition's politics is that they are fighting with the image of the RSS which is not its reality. The RSS is morphing day by day and the image the opposition parties are attacking is much older and has become obsolete. These parties are, in fact, attacking the shadow of the RSS but are unable to understand the real RSS for their mobilization.

A few opposition leaders have now decided to fight the RSS with its own weapon. West Bengal chief minister and Trinamool Congress (TMC) supremo, Mamata Banerjee, announced the formation of two new outfits—Jai Hind Vahini and Bang Janani Samiti—reportedly to fight the influence of the RSS in the state. Banerjee said the two wings would fight to keep Bengal's political environment secular.[20] Former Congress president Rahul Gandhi too has been targeting the RSS and the BJP, saying that his fight with the two is ideological.[21] The question, however, is which RSS are the two leaders actually taking on?

The RSS that Gandhi and Banerjee are claiming to fight, existed thirty to forty years back, while the RSS of today is a drastically changed organization. To fight this new RSS, these two leaders need to understand the changes that have appeared in the RSS ideology. To take on the RSS, political parties like the Congress and the TMC need to create a new body and soul. They need to create new organizations. These organizations will show that they are not only there for the politics of power and state, but to usher in a politics of social change. A strategy that RSS leaders have successfully applied is the notion of *tyag* (renunciation). The RSS mobilizes communities but does not claim power and money for itself. If the volunteers find someone suitable for politics among themselves, they send that person to join the BJP. They don't put their own relatives into any organization. The notion of tyag attracts Indian people and strikes a chord with them. These are traditional cultural values that are rooted in the people's psyche. The RSS produces a corpus of pracharaks who have renounced their families and have dedicated their lives to its ideology. On the other hand, Mamata Banerjee appointed her brother in the organizations that she formed to fight against the RSS. So, Banerjee lost the battle even before it began— she lost the battle of gaining people's trust. The RSS is able to exert its strength because of its cultural rooting and location. Parties like the Congress and TMC need to evolve a counter hegemony through a new cultural politics.

No cultural politics can begin with an organization that does not understand Indian traditions and society. They can fight with the BJP, but it will be very difficult for them to combat the RSS, which is the womb of the power of Hindutva politics. The RSS is now no longer an organization where the volunteers wield spears or sticks. The volunteers today wield a far more powerful weapon, which is the mission of creating a sociocultural hegemony that would include the entire Hindu community and even many traditionally non-Hindu tribals and other minority groups. They are armed with smartphones, advance communication technology and the power of social media. It will be very difficult to counter the RSS ideology with the outmoded language of secularism and conventional party organization. People need to see the real RSS instead of its old shadow. Criticism of its organization-based violence and hollow talk cannot defeat the RSS, because the outfit has the strength of appropriation and inclusion.

2

APPROPRIATION AS PROCESS

Caste, Dalits and Hindutva

*Hé Purush Sinh, tum bhi yah shakti karo dharan
Aradhan ka dridh aradhan se do uttar*

—Suryakant Tripathi 'Nirala'[1]

(O lion among men! Attire yourself in power,
return worship with unwavering worship)

*Sangh desh ke 130 karor ki abaadi ko Hindu samaj
maanta hai. Bharat me rahne-wala har nagrik,
chahe wah kisi bhi dharm ya sanskriti ka ho, uske
andar rashtravad ki bhavana hai aur wah Bharat ki
sanskriti ka samman karta hai . . . wah kisi dharm
ka ho, kisi bhi tarah se puja kare ya na kare, wah
Hindu hai. Yah poora samaj hamara hai. Sangh ka
lakshya akhand samaj banana hai.*

—Mohan Bhagwat, Sarsanghchalak, the RSS[2]

(The Sangh considers the country's 130 crore people Hindus. All residents of India, whichever religion or culture they belong to, have the sentiment of nationalism and respect India's culture. . . . Whichever religion they are from, however they pray or don't pray, they are Hindu. This entire society is ours. The objective of the Sangh is to form a united society.)

Resistance and appropriation are the two tactics that work in the domain of power as both provide space for political expansion. Hindutva politics works on the strategic process of appropriation very effectively. If someone watches closely how the BJP and the RSS function in tandem, one will find that they increase their influence through the modes of appropriation. At the core of this strategy lie the groups which had been, until recently, antagonized by both the RSS and the BJP. These are marginalized groups like tribals, Dalits, women and minorities.

Between 1980 and 1990, the Sangh established a *seva prabhag* (service cell) that launched various projects among tribals and

Dalits, and in the North-eastern states. Drawing its inspiration from the great figure of Swami Vivekananda,[3] it also started to perform *seva karya* (service work) during natural disasters, such as floods, earthquakes, etc. However, the Sangh may have evolved seva as a strategy of deepening its organization, in response to the Christian missionaries and their social service projects in the impoverished zones of India.

Now both the RSS and the BJP have started to co-opt these social groups, and the Sangh and its affiliates are already working in these social pockets under various names and banners. This appropriation is not merely a symbolic one of contesting identities, but is based on hard work on various development-related issues through social projects. Hindutva-centred mass organizations have launched these projects in the interior areas and among marginal communities in the recent past. Some of these projects have been undertaken through the samrasta campaign, and organizations such as Vanvasi Kalyan Ashram, Bharatiya Stree Shakti and Vaibhav Shree. Through seva karya in hard times, times of natural disasters, the RSS and its allied organizations provide support to people, which makes space for their ideology in the minds and hearts of the affected.[4]

Muslim Rashtriya Manch, various tribal welfare (*vanvasi kalyan*) groups, samarasta campaign groups and the Rashtriya Sevika Samiti are some of these RSS-affiliated groups working effectively with different social sections. In the understanding of the RSS, these sections are the soft targets of radical politics, including Ambedkarite politics and Naxalism, and of political parties like the Communist Party of India (Marxist) or CPM, the BSP and, to some extent, the Congress.[5] Along with the RSS, the BJP too has been making inroads in these pockets, while the RSS and its affiliated organizations are already working among these communities to provide them education, health, employment, and so on; these organizations are autonomous and not connected to the government. However, when the RSS cadres first enter tribal or Dalit localities, it is difficult for them to gain the faith of the community. Being from outside the community, they are seen with suspicion and their motives come under question. Another difficulty they face is where and how to set the level of interaction with the community. Thus, the process of doing seva karya is very complex and imbued with various tensions.

Hindutva groups require a broad-based Hindu support to succeed electorally. This means the subsuming of caste identity into a larger religious framework and the promotion of a Hindu community with shared interests that rises above caste considerations. This religious identity becomes the basis of mobilizing votes; the campaign rhetoric is designed to persuade voters that while Hindus may have internal differences, exacerbated by caste, they must unite for their greater common good. Of course, caste is a system of social hierarchy. A growing consciousness in independent India of the inequities of caste, and a growing political voice, has meant that Dalit and OBC (Other Backward Class) communities are less fearful of rejecting the system. They embrace the politics of opposing caste discrimination, an assertion of their rights and entitlements in a secular society in which, theoretically, everyone is equal and everyone deserves the opportunity to succeed.

'Caste politics', as it is popularly known, catalysed by the implementation of the recommendations of the Mandal Commission report, seemed, until 2014, to be inherently inimical to the politics of Hindutva, as if the latter was only for the upper castes. Gradually, electoral concerns compelled the political parties espousing Hindutva to accommodate the politics of caste assertion. Hindutva had to appropriate caste assertion and reposition caste identity from *dharmparayan* (follower of religion) to *dharmrakshak* (saviour of religion). It is easy for Hindutva politics to mobilize the upper castes on grounds of nationalism allied to religion, but an altogether more rigorous discourse was needed to appropriate the various OBC and Dalit communities that are deeply suspicious of the 'Brahminical' value system which they link to Hindutva. The RSS is trying to bring these communities within the Hindutva fold; it envisions a gradual fading away of caste identity by evolving a broader Hindu identity among everyone—poor to rich, and Dalits and tribal groups to higher castes. The current RSS chief, Mohan Bhagwat, in his recent meeting with the pracharaks of Meerut, Braj and Uttarakhand, appealed to them to work to unite the marginalized of our society within the Hindu fold by encouraging the feeling of Hindutva among them, such that their caste identity becomes insignificant.[6]

Dealing with Dalit Castes

The attempt to expand public spaces by giving these a Hindutva meaning is a new strategy adopted by the BJP. The BJP is working on the discursive ground prepared by the RSS to mobilize Dalits towards Hindutva. For this, the RSS explored and reinvented the heroes of almost every Dalit caste to mobilize each one individually by evoking its unique identity. The party reinterpreted and recreated the cultural resources of Dalits at the local level, including their caste histories and memories, with the aim of adding a sense of Hindutva identity to their psyche, ultimately transforming them into sites for political mobilization. The folklore of various marginalized castes, particularly Dalits, have been selected by the RSS and the party in different regions to incorporate these into a single, unified Hindutva metanarrative.

One of the ways to do this was to glorify the various caste heroes as Hindu warriors. Hindutva organizations would fund *jayanti* (anniversary) celebrations of these heroes, install their statues and treat them as icons beyond their caste identities. One such is Suheldeo, whom the Pasi Rajbhar caste considers their hero. Realizing the political and electoral importance of the Pasis, an important Dalit community in north India, the RSS launched a campaign to project Suheldeo as a Hindu hero because he allegedly defeated a Ghaznavid general. And this community was projected as a Rashtra Rakshak Shiromani (the greatest saviour of the nation) for defending

Hindu culture and the country from Muslim intruders. Festivals were organized in memory of Suheldeo in Chittora. Thus the RSS and the BJP projected this Dalit caste as the militia or saviours who make up the army of protectors of Hindu dharma.[7]

The RSS also celebrated other Pasi heroes such as Baldeo and Daldeo, who were once used by parties like the BSP, which was formed by Kanshiram in 1984 as a party exclusively for the backward castes and minority groups. These figures, earlier projected as symbolic Dalit heroes who resisted upper-caste oppression, were now being transformed into 'national', 'Hindu' heroes by the RSS.[8] Some examples of co-opted Dalit heroes are Ravidas and Supach Rishi from the Jatav community; Dina-Bhadri, worshipped by the Musahar community as deities for fighting for the rights of bonded labourers; Ahir hero Lorik Yadav; and, perhaps most famously, Sardar Vallabhbhai Patel (from the Kurmi community) who, according to Hindutva lore, has been denied his due in national mainstream politics.[9] To create a connection with these communities, the BJP-led NDA (National Democratic Alliance) government even named a new 'superfast' express train from Ghazipur to Delhi after Suheldeo.[10] Hindutva politics cleverly merged caste icons with wider national heroes, managing to combine India, Hinduism and Hindutva into a single seamless idea. This strategy of the RSS to appropriate lower-caste heroes helped bring Dalit and OBC voters in the state of UP over to the BJP and enabled the party to sweep the parliamentary polls in 2014 with 282 seats while the BJP-led NDA acquired 336 seats.

Alongside, the RSS has worked hard in non-Jatav Dalit communities and among non-Yadav OBCs in the Hindi belt. It has also worked with tribals, nomads and other marginalized castes in tribal zones from Gujarat to Tripura. The project was always to mobilize the political potential of these groups in UP, MP, Rajasthan, Chhattisgarh and Jharkhand and to convert the seva of the Parivar into valuable votes. In time, the BJP appears to have succeeded in combining caste consciousness with Hindutva consciousness, to change the emphasis from resisting caste oppression to singing the glories and legends of caste history within the fold of Hinduism. Hindutva discourses reinterpret the history, identities, resources, symbols and cultures of communities and link them to a Hindu metanarrative of the Vedas, the Puranas and Ram. This metanarrative tries to project itself as equivalent to the 'nation' or 'national interests', within which it further incorporates caste. This is why, during the campaign for the 2019 elections, the rhetoric of the BJP leaders on Pulwama, Balakot and national security was barely distinguishable from their narrative on the Ram temple. The fight against terrorism and creation of the temple, it appears, were the core of the BJP agenda, even if 'development' was the buzzword in the 2014 elections.

During the 2019 general elections, the BJP created a mix of nationalist and Hindutva tropes, alongside a more muted appeal to the aspiration for development. The BJP had also formed alliances with caste-based parties to garner SC and OBC votes. Take, for instance, the alliance with Apna Dal, led by Union minister Anupriya Patel (of Kurmi caste in UP) or the Suheldev Bharatiya Samaj Party led by Om Prakash Rajbhar, a UP minister influential in the state's east. The same considerations underline the links with Nitish Kumar and Ram Vilas Paswan in Bihar. Upper-caste Hindus are largely on board with Hindutva as an ideology and they buy the political and cultural logic of the RSS. Many Vaishya communities too would count themselves as the BJP's base. But assimilating the Dalits of UP and Bihar within Hindutva has been the biggest challenge for the RSS and the BJP. A broad caste coalition was stitched up in 2014, but there have been significant upheavals since.

The BJP's relations with the various Dalit castes are tense and complex. For the party, Dalit assertiveness has been difficult to comprehend, let alone accept. The BJP is trying hard to accommodate Dalit groups, but it knows that this embrace is not palatable to its core supporters. Until the early 1980s, before the Ram Janmabhoomi movement, in northern and western India, the BJP was always seen as a party of the urban middle class, the Banias and a section of Brahmins. Over time, the party also brought several OBCs and MBCs within its fold. With the retreat of socialist politics that started around that period, the rural neo-rich from among the OBCs began to feel marginalized in national politics and moved towards Hindutva politics.[11] From the 1970s to 1990s, these communities purchased rural land at a much faster rate and emerged as a landed community. On one hand, this affluent group appears to be part of the new political leadership for post-Mandal Hindutva politics, while on the other, being a landed community, it is also perceived to be the oppressor of Dalits in everyday rural life. This complicates matters for the BJP, which is now trying to bring them together in the party.

Another campaign launched by the BJP and the RSS in recent years has been to initiate nationwide activities to integrate Dalits and upper castes by arranging community meals, opening schools in Dalit settlements, and organizing sensitization campaigns for upper castes. This has its beginnings in the early 1980s, when the samajik samrasta campaign was launched in Maharashtra. Its primary objective was to eradicate internal conflicts among Hindus while its second aim was to assimilate Dalits into the mainstream by providing them with health, educational and entrepreneurial assistance. A crucial move was to invite Dalits to eat khichri with the upper castes; it was attended by several of the RSS cadres and BJP workers, including a number of upper-caste members. Another initiative was the establishment of the Samajik Samrasta Manch on the occasion of Ambedkar Jayanti on 14 April 1983.

In addition to these strategies, the Sangh Parivar also began to propagate the concept of Ramarajya (literally, 'the rule of Ram', implies a regime of high morals) in which the upper and lower castes come together in social life as well as in democratic politics. For instance, the Ramayana and Lord Ram have been projected as symbols of unity by contending to Dalits that

Ram was always linked to the downtrodden and that the epic centred on the Dalits. According to this viewpoint, Dalits played a significant role in Ram's life story, in the quest to find his wife, Sita, in Lanka. The roles of Sugriva, Angada, Jambavan, Hanuman and his army, all symbolizing the underprivileged, were crucial in the Ramayana, according to the Sangh and BJP ideologues. This reveals the Sangh's attempt to absorb growing Dalit dissent against Brahminism as well as their struggle for self-respect and equality, by transforming the newly emerging Dalit–Bahujan identity into a Hindutva one. 'Bahujan' was a term initially coined by Gautam Buddha. It was also widely used in Maharashtra politics. While forming the Bahujan Samaj Party, Kanshiram used this term to bring together all the backward castes under a single, unified identity.

The BJP has redoubled its efforts to appropriate B.R. Ambedkar, as is evident from the recent inauguration of several memorials.[12] Also, prior to the 2014 Lok Sabha elections in Bihar and UP, the BJP president Amit Shah took part in caste rallies and meetings of various Dalit communities. A big dilemma for the RSS and the BJP is that they are willing to assimilate Dalits within their fold but on their own terms. After Independence, due to various state-led developmental efforts, a literate, critical-minded Dalit leadership has emerged. These leaders are inspired by the writings of Periyar E.V. Ramasami, Jyotiba Phule and Ambedkar, and their consciousness is informed by a trenchant criticism of Hinduism and Hindutva ideology. Though a small part of this group is under the BJP's influence, it is also influenced by Ambedkarite thought. The RSS has not yet come to terms with this. A deep churning is going on within Hindutva politics about how to accommodate these Ambedkarite Dalit leaders in Hindutva-led power politics, both symbolic and real.

It is this situation that leads to clashes in educational institutions between students charged with Ambedkarite consciousness and those belonging to Sangh-affiliated organizations. Clashes could also occur with the belligerent middle castes—who have become influential in recent decades under the BJP leadership—as it may not be easy for them to accept the assertion of the Dalit groups. All this also causes tension within Sangh organizations. Thus, a conflict between Ambedkarite consciousness and Hindutva consciousness over religion, politics and society has become even more violent with the emergence of state power. After coming to power, the BJP is trying to resolve this tussle administratively. The biggest challenge before the Sangh Parivar in the politics of Dalit appropriation is the clash of ideas. In the process of the RSS and the BJP trying to subsume Dalit ideas under the larger narratives of Hindutva, nationalism and development, it is not only the young Ambedkarites who are under attack; the Sangh organizations too are getting hurt.

Appropriating Religious Sects

In addition to co-opting Dalit and lower-caste heroes into the Hindutva fold, the BJP has been appropriating religious symbols and icons associated with popular sects, such as the Nath Panth, Ravidassias and the Kabir Panth, as these sects have a large following among the Dalits, MBCs and OBCs. The party is also trying to correlate Hindu symbols with those of Buddhism in order to mobilize Buddhists, many of whom belong to the Dalit and OBC communities. This strategy aims to do two things. One, provide respect to icons who are key to the Dalit desire for dignity. Two, forge linkages between Hindutva and the popular sects, which were expressions of non- and anti-Brahminical upsurges at different times in the country's history. A key purpose of this strategy is to gain the trust of the Dalits and marginal communities. These strategies, while ongoing, are stepped up when certain upheavals take place, in order to recover lost ground; for instance, this was done after Rohith Vemula's suicide in 2016, some very visible cases of atrocities and the bitterness over the reservation issue in 2020.[13]

On 26 June 2018, Prime Minister Narendra Modi visited Maghar, the place where Kabir was cremated, to observe the 620th Prakatya Diwas and the 500th death anniversary of Kabir. He laid the foundation of the Kabir International Academy, conceived as a study, research, publication and exhibition complex devoted to Kabir's life and teachings. The prime minister's speech underscored how the symbol of Ram was important to Kabir. This is how the BJP is trying to woo the Kabirpanthis and draw them towards Hindutva. The communities of Julahas, Tantis, Kovids, Koris and Jogis, who live in a region stretching from Punjab to Bihar and Bengal, are known to be traditional followers of the Kabir Panth. They are called 'Vayanjeevi', the conglomeration of weaver communities. The Kabir Panth later became popular among the Jatavs and MBC and OBC castes in UP, Bihar and MP. In UP, about half of the Jatav community could be Kabirpanthis and the rest are followers of Ravidassia sects. Kabir is also venerated by backward agrarian castes like Kurmis, Kushwahas, Kunjars and Paneris.[14]

The cultural artefacts centred on Kabir, like rhymes and folk songs, are also popular among a wide section of the rural population. Marginal Muslim socio-religious groups also associate with the symbolism around Kabir. In many UP villages, the same Kabir song could be sung in a Jatav *chaupal* (meeting) or a Brahmin *baithak* (congregation). Weaver communities such as the Koris, who are part of the Hindu fold, and Ansaris who are Muslims, are known to support the BSP and Samajwadi Party (Socialist Party; SP) in UP, especially in the areas adjoining Gorakhpur and Varanasi—both large electoral constituencies. By appropriating Kabir, the BJP hopes to get these communities to vote for it. UP Chief Minister Yogi Adityanath has already emerged as a strong Hindutva icon who can mobilize Nathpanthis in different parts of India.

This politics of symbols does not only help the BJP build up a vote bank, but also helps the party develop a cadre base comprising people of these sects. In the 2018 elections to the Karnataka Assembly, cadres drawn from the Nathpanthis and some other religious sects worked for the BJP. Kabirpanthi maths usually keep photographs of Kabir and Ambedkar. So, the maths of these sects are also instrumental in building the political consciousness of their followers. At times, they influence their electoral behaviour. In the 1990s, Kabirpanthi maths were sources of goodwill for Kanshiram, Mayawati and the BSP. Kabirpanthi mahants, such as Garbu Goswami from Siwan, have also contested elections in UP and Bihar.

Modi also visited a temple dedicated to Ravidas in Varanasi, to participate in Ravidas Jayanti celebrations on 19 February 2019. He had also participated in these celebrations in 2016. Ravidas is a very powerful religious figure for Dalit communities. He is worshipped by them as their deity, saint and guru who showed them the path of bhakti and struggled to provide them space in the religious and spiritual domain. He is also remembered as an icon who inspired them to fight for equality and justice. He is revered by the community as a *gyani* (wise man) who created a religious and social discourse to ensure dignity to the Untouchables and lower castes. Large sections of Dalit communities all over India, especially in the north, are part of the Ravidassia sect. They are also asserting to get Ravidassia dharm recognized as a separate religion. A large section of the Jatav community, the largest group among Dalits in the north, relate themselves to the Ravidassia sect. One may find small or big temples in many *basti*s (settlements) of north India revered by Dalit communities, especially Jatavs, cobblers and Dhusiya. Interestingly, most of the Dalits of north India revere Kabir, Ravidas and Ambedkar together. If one visits Ravidas temples, in some of them one may also find calendars or photographs of Ambedkar on the walls, along with the statue of Ravidas. Thus, the symbol of Ravidas was originally a socio-religious one, but has slowly extended to become one of social and political awareness. He is now closely linked with the identity and sense of social empowerment for the Dalits. Understanding this fact, the effort of the BJP and Hindutva politics to link themselves with the symbol of Ravidas is a well-thought-out strategy to expand their base among Dalit communities.

Hindutva among Tribal Communities

Bringing the tribal communities living in different parts of India within the fold of Hindutva is a great challenge for the RSS and the BJP, since they form a sizeable population and consequently a big vote bank. For long, certain tribal zones of India have remained under the influence of either Christian missionaries or Naxalites. In the late seventeenth and early eighteenth centuries, tribals in North-eastern, central and eastern India came under the influence of the Christian missionaries who had arrived along with the British. These Christian missionaries worked for the betterment of the lives of the tribals. After India became independent, the missionaries stayed on and continued to work for the tribal communities. But the tribals could not find a dignified space in our democratic politics, even after

Independence. Tribal areas, known for their rich natural resources, were affected by the building of industries, dams, hydroelectricity projects as a part of national development. But instead of benefiting from such projects, they were largely displaced and excluded from the dividends of their own resources. The missionaries supported the movements for their rights.[15] But the real conflict began when in the 1990s Hindu organizations started working among them more intensively and accused the Christians of misguiding them against national and Hindu identity.

In late 1970s and early 1980s, the RSS quietly started to enter tribal zones in MP, Jharkhand and Chhattisgarh, and their efforts at the grassroots have started showing results. Apart from the political significance of the move, it created a counter to the Christian proselytizing activities as well. A section of the population was also stopped from turning into Naxal sympathizers. It made similar moves in the North-east from around the time of Independence. The shift has proved decisive for the BJP's electoral victories. From Gujarat to the North-east, the most recent elections have indicated a trend of tribal votes shifting towards the BJP in a very impressive way.[16] Media reports, researchers and political observers are of the view that this shift is due to the relentless work the RSS has been doing in the tribal areas. Even analysts who are usually hesitant to give any credit to the RSS for the BJP's electoral gains, are beginning to recognize its contribution in this area.

The intervention of the Sangh and its affiliated organizations among the tribals in India is not new. During the 1930s, many princely states passed an anti-conversion law in tribal zones. The activities of the missionaries and the rise in conversion of tribals to Christianity created situations in which Hindutva organizations got the space to work among tribal people. During the 1950s, the Vanvasi Kalyan Ashram, an allied organization of the RSS, began working in central India, especially MP and Chhattisgarh. It launched various projects in the areas of health, education and livelihood. Through these projects it has been slowly expanding its reach among tribal communities. It is working hard to reshape the tribal identity as the vanvasi identity, as opposed to the Adivasi identity.[17] The RSS and its affiliates also launched the *paravartan* (reconversion) campaign that 'reconverted' converted tribals to Hindu religion or to their indigenous faith.[18] In this way, the RSS is not only reshaping the religious consciousness of the tribals, but is also gradually trying to rebuild their political consciousness. The RSS's intervention among tribal people in MP, Jharkhand and Chhattisgarh slowly weakened the Congress's stronghold among them. This resulted in a major shift of tribal voting patterns in favour of the BJP in the last few parliamentary and Assembly elections, notably in 2014 and 2019.[19] The growing influence of the RSS in tribal zones has made many stalwart tribal leaders of the Congress irrelevant, even in their own areas of influence.

Among the strategies employed by the RSS for this purpose was that it formed NGOs to work among the tribals, to drive them towards the Sangh, and to empower them as 'respectable citizens'. The Hindutva-inspired NGOs started various social work projects among the tribal communities, such as creating infrastructure for good health facilities, opening schools and colleges, building temples as social–religious spaces in the villages, and so on. Alongside, the RSS has set up free schools with hostel facilities in remote areas where state facilities have not yet reached. These schools and textbooks are based on the RSS's own pedagogy for tribes. Similarly, they came up with many *aarogyashala*s (hospitals of ayurveda, homeopathy and modern medicine) there. In an attempt to support the indigenous knowledge of the tribal communities, the RSS institutes started imparting training in archery, wrestling and other traditional sports, to enable them to compete in national-level competitions. Thus, while on one hand, the Sangh attracted the tribals through seva, on the other hand, it tried to cultivate a Hindu identity among them.

The training imparted by the RSS to the children completely transforms them and later they become role models for their communities. A Sangh pracharak working among the tribals in Sonebhadra area of UP said: 'These boys also learn bhajan–kirtan and moral education from our schools. After passing from our schools, they go to cities and we support their higher education too. We maintain an ongoing relationship with them.'[20] The Sangh believes in the traditional ways of tribal living. There is an acute water crisis in many tribal areas. The Vanvasi Kalyan Ashram in Sonebhadra has thus taken up a project to revive traditional sources of water to address the shortage. An activist explained how they are also concentrating on reviving tribal businesses. Students from nearby technical schools or business schools are often invited to exchange ideas to develop avenues for tribal livelihood, which conform to their tradition and culture.[21]

Setting up temples of Hanuman or statues of other Hindu gods and goddesses is also part of the RSS's outreach project. At some places, many other Hindu organizations are also chipping in to reconstruct a tribal culture.

Tribal deities are placed inside Hindu temples as well, forging a Hindu–tribal synergy. 'Both societies have the same values and moral structures. We are working to explore such links, which may create unity in the society.'[22] The RSS is also working to produce an impressive number of pracharaks from tribal communities and using them to expand the shakha network in the tribal zones of central India, as well as in the rest of the country.

Saffron Slums

Once Ambedkar had opined that Indian villages are like a slaughterhouse for Dalits, where they suffer various kinds of oppression by the dominant castes. That they should leave villages and migrate to the cities.[23] However when Dalits and other marginalized groups migrate to the cities and the urban sphere for their livelihood, they mostly settle in the slums for lack of resources. According to the 2011 Census, around 17.36 per cent of India's urban population lives in the slums of various cities, towns and districts. In UP, India's largest state, the population of slum dwellers is around 14.02 per cent, with most of them belonging to Dalit and other marginalized and poor communities. These slums present a fertile ground for the flourishing of Hindutva politics. According to popular perception, it is assumed that they desire and fight for houses, jobs, ration cards, government-supported medical treatment and monetary aid, and so on. However, they also aspire for small temples where they can worship, assemble in the evening and share their joys and sorrows with neighbours. This means they also desire their own public and religious space. In other words, along with economic betterment and enhancement of the quality of life, slum dwellers also want religious empowerment. And, each passing day, they are embracing the Hindu religious identity.

It is no wonder that the RSS and its various affiliates have started entering these slums with their seva campaigns, such as opening schools and organizing medical camps. The RSS shakhas are also expanding in these slums and trying to emphasize their identity as Indian Hindus. They also organize entertainment programmes for slum dwellers like football matches and *kabaddi* competitions. So, one may clearly observe the efforts by the RSS towards transforming the identity of slum dwellers from 'poor' to 'Hindu' or one that suffixes 'Hindu' to 'poor'. Many Hindutva-based small organizations, such as Hindu Yuva Vahini, Hindu Rakshak Sangh, and so on, have started working in slums in various cities of UP.[24] There is a new trend worth noting here. On one hand, the RSS and its affiliates like the VHP, Sanskar Bharati, Hind Mazdoor Sabha, Bharat Vikas Parishad, Sahakar Bharati, Pragya Pravah and several others, are targeting these slums.[25] On the other hand, several unofficial Hindutva-oriented outfits have suddenly emerged in these social locations. These have been launched by a few politically ambitious local leaders, who may or may not have had any connection with Hindutva politics previously, but have now formed small distinct groups to acquire political value. The former are working in the slums with their strategies of seva and *sahyog* (cooperation), while the newer outfits are trying to mobilize these populations under an aggressive Hindutva Identity. The difference lies in the discourse. The RSS attempts to reshape their identity as Hindu citizens by inspiring them to absorb various Hindu *sanskara*s (customs), but these smaller outfits are trying to transform the slum dwellers into *garvonnat* (proud) Hindus. The tone and tenor of these campaigns are producing two kinds of political cultures. Sometimes, the two overlap, but they generate two distinct streams of Hindutva identity. One is posturing as a 'soft' Hindu, while the other positions itself as the proponent of an aggressive or assertive Hindu.

It is interesting to know that sometimes the RSS appears uncomfortable with the presence and growing influence of these small aggressive Hindutva outfits. The RSS faces some difficulties in handling them, often leading to conflict and contestation between these two groups. It is true that both these groups are producing a political ambience that may give political benefits to the BJP, but Hindutva subjectivities they generate are different. One wants to appropriate others within its own Hindutva framework; the other doesn't want to tolerate a different identity and culture. While there is a fine line between the two political cultures emerging in the slums of UP, both work separately. Some people from the smaller groups may have joined an RSS shakha at some point in their life, but now they have evolved their own ways.[26]

Earlier, slums were considered spaces for leftist and radical Ambedkarite politics, but now their political demography is changing very fast. Kanshiram, during the period of 1980s to '90s, tried to evolve these sites as the base area for Bahujan politics—and succeeded to an extent—but now it is turning into a space for Hindutva politics. The transformation from the 'BSP blue' to 'Hindutva saffron' is happening rapidly. Their economic aspiration is being linked to their religious aspiration. Since Hindutva social, cultural and political groups use religious identity as an important resource in their mobilizational campaign, they are building up their influence over the newly emerging aspirations of the poor, which is linked to religious empowerment.[27] Now, one can often hear the chants of *sunderkand paath* from the Ramayana and also of Hanuman Chalisa recitations rising from well-organized programmes in these slums. The RSS is also working to build small temples of Hindu deities here. Both these kinds of Hindutva organisations are alert to the possibility of religious conversion of the underprivileged, and claim that their work is an antidote to that. They claim that their efforts contribute to the strengthening of Hindu society.

Listening and Appropriating

The RSS, through its samajik samrasta campaign sends its cadres to visit villages and hamlets and instructs them to sit with the *vanchit–ativanchit* (underprivileged and extremely marginalized) social groups, eat with them, spend time and listen to their personal stories, and try to understand their desires, dreams and aspirations. The RSS has trained its cadres not to speak like politicians but to listen to these groups with empathy and compassion. Listening is a good strategy to create space within the target group and ultimately bring them within their fold. In the previous chapter, too, we saw how this works. One RSS cadre working in the Shankargarh area near Prayagraj told me: *'Jodana aur judne ke liye sunana zaroori hai.'* (It is necessary to listen to link and join with them.)[28]

During my studies on marginalized and Dalit communities in north India, I realized that there is a sense of anguish within them that no one listens to them. An old Dalit woman in a village near Prayagraj said with deep pain to my research team: 'No one listens to us as we are poor.'[29]

We heard an interesting narrative in a Mushahar village near Sasaram in Bihar, which exposed the schisms between the most vulnerable sections of the Indian public and the politicians, academicians and policymakers. An old man told us: *'Bhaiyya, yeh saheb, suba, malik-hakim, mantri-santri log ya toh humein sunte nahi; sunte hain toh samajhate nahi; samajhte bhi toh jo hum chahte hain uska theek ulta karate hai.'* (Brother, these sahibs, overseers of administrative zones, doctors, ministers, etc., either don't listen to us; even if they listen, they don't understand us; and even when they understand, they do just the opposite of what we want.) This common complaint in rural areas reveals how ignorant our politicians and policymakers are of the buried desires of the marginalized. Due to this, there is a disconnect at multiple levels. Politicians tend to listen only to assertive communities. They don't listen to or understand communities that are small in number and appear to be meek and mild.

In UP, around sixty-six communities are mentioned as SC communities. Together they are also called Dalits. However, most people are only aware of a few communities from that list, such as Jatavs, Pasi, Kori, Valmiki, etc. More than fifty Dalit communities are suffering because they are not at the forefront of the Dalit castes. Castes like Hari, Beggar, Vanmanush,

Tatwa, Kuchbadhiya, Kabutra, Musahars, etc., are not yet 'politically visible' in UP. Similarly, in Maharashtra, only a few Dalit communities like Mahars, Matang, Mang, Chambhar, etc., are well known. Similarly, in Andhra Pradesh more than fifty communities are mentioned in the SC list, but most people only know castes like Mala and Madiga. In an electoral democracy like ours, only the castes that hold electoral value in terms of vote are heard by political leaders and parties. All the states have lists of the Scheduled Castes, but only those castes are known that are big in number and have acquired the capacity to assert their voices due to various historical reasons. This is why most Dalit communities are not part of our political and public discourse.

One of the important reasons behind the invisibility of these small Dalit castes is that they are scattered in their settlements and are unable to form a consolidated section of voters. Secondly, most of them do not have an educated section among them to write and speak for them. Many of them have not yet produced community leaders nor their own politics. Some have also not evolved their caste histories in terms of their caste identity. There are a few who are trying to enter the politics of local self-government in UP but they haven't yet produced members of Parliament (MPs) or members of the Legislative Assembly (MLAs) from their own caste. It is appalling and disturbing to see that many of these 'invisible' Dalit communities do not even aspire for a good life.

One RSS cadre shared his experience of interacting with people of marginalized communities in Prayagraj and emphasized the need for empathy. This empathy was also expressed in metaphors like *par kaya pravesh* (entering the body of others). He added that one needs to develop *sukh-dukh sambandh* (relationship of sharing joy and sorrow) with the marginalized, so that they may open up and narrate their wishes and desires. He further said that they usually sent those cadres to the samrasta programmes who belonged to the oppressed castes so that they could easily connect with the target communities. He also told us that their intention is that the cadres try to understand their language. By this he meant the language of the heart and mind of the downtrodden, not just the language spoken by the people.[30]

Listening to the marginalized is an art that even many of our social activists—well-meaning but distant due to their western education—and politicians are yet to cultivate. There is also a strong need to understand the folk dialects as well as the silences and murmurs of these communities. The RSS is trying to wedge itself into this fallow space and, through that, associate with these communities. It prepares a mental make-up of these communities, which helps the BJP forge a political relationship with them.

3

FORGING A NEW MOBILIZATIONAL CONSCIOUSNESS

'Because things are the way they are, things
will not stay the way they are'

—Bertolt Brecht

I begin this chapter with the statement of an
RSS cadre working in Kashi district, who
says: 'We don't want any communal riot
in society . . . it hampers the growth of our
organization.'[1] I have found similar opinions
being expressed in my interactions with several
local RSS cadres during my extensive fieldwork
in UP over many years. It is true that the
sociopolitical conditions that emerge out of the
RSS groundwork are often used by Hindutva

political agencies, such as Ram Rajya Parishad, the BJP and the Shiv Sena, for a certain kind of mobilization during elections.[2] But the RSS pracharaks opine that the blame of communal riots damages their credibility and reputation, which they acquire through hard work.

All democratic systems exert constant pressure on political parties to mobilize people for electoral purposes. Electoral mobilization is often based on evoking emotive issues such as religion, language, caste and parochialism. Development and other rational issues also get transformed into emotional issues because of the unequal distribution of resources and opportunities, and people's growing expectations. A study of the history of elections in Indian democracy would show that religion and caste have consistently been the most effective planks for mobilization by different political parties.

In the 1990s, both the politics of religious mobilization around the Ramjanambhoomi– Babri Masjid issue and the caste-based politics that emerged after the implementation of the Mandal Commission report, were strengthened and became very powerful. The SP and BSP in UP and the Rashtriya Janata Dal (National People's Party; RJD) in Bihar emerged around caste politics. To counter this caste mobilization the BJP moved ahead around religious identities. Since then, this political strategy has been used to neutralize and diffuse caste politics. Several times, the issues of caste assertion remained active even after being subsumed within the larger purview of religion, and often the rise of middle and Dalit caste identities worked against communal politics. These two issues have not remained opposed to each other, but work together to take a complex form of electoral mobilization. Thus, both caste consciousness (*jatibhav*) and communal consciousness (*sampradiyikbhav*) have proved necessary for various political parties depending on time and electoral compulsions. Often both caste and communal consciousness join with politics and become aggressive in their outer and inner forms, in their appearance and substance, and in their process and consequence. The BJP as a political member of the Hindtuva family introduced a new turn of identity politics in the 2014 parliamentary elections through a combination of the desire for development and a consciousness based on religious identity—this completely shattered the dichotomy between communal and caste identity that had hitherto existed in Indian politics and society. They had understood that religious identity–based politics will not succeed by itself but had to be linked with the desire for development that had arisen in the minds of common people, particularly from the underprivileged castes, who were battling with underdevelopment. They successfully combined these two elements while devising a strategy for mobilizing people of all castes and communities, including Muslims, to vote for them. For instance, during the Assembly election in UP in 2017, the BJP tried to subsume Dalit identity within the Hindu identity and raised issues that were relatable to both the upper-caste and Dalit Hindus. At a political rally in Fatehpur during his election campaign on 19 February 2017, PM Modi said, 'If you create a *kabristaan* (graveyard) in a village, then a *shamshaan* (cremation ground) should be created. If electricity is given uninterrupted in Ramzan, then it should be given in Diwali without a break. *Bhedbhaav nahin hona chahiye* [There should be no discrimination].'[3] It is the Dalits who work in Hindu cremation grounds, and by raising this issue, the BJP offered them a sense of inclusion.

The Phenomenon of Small Clashes

It is well known that communal riots don't occur, they are engineered; and the people engineering these riots have certain motives that are usually guided by political mobilization and electoral interest.[4] If one were to study the history of the forms of communal riots in the post-Independence period, one would find several changes in them over time and space. Leaving aside the riots that erupted during Partition, historians and social scientists have always considered communal riots as a phenomenon occurring in the urban space. However, in the post-liberalization era in India, after the early 1990s, communal clashes started to spread in villages as well. The second change that has now occurred is that whereas earlier there used to be big communal riots after long intervals, now different religious groups are being mobilized on an ongoing basis over an extended period of time. The politically ambitious outfits that have emerged after the BJP's rise to power have started to mobilize people around religious identities by creating small incidents of conflict. These small clashes, which are mostly invisible, sporadic and latent, cannot be called 'riots' and yet have a deeper and longer-lasting impact. Some fringe outfits mobilize the Hindus, while criminal elements associated with certain parties mobilize Muslims, often without the parties' approval.[5] Through this new strategy, communal consciousness is no longer momentary but has become a continuous presence, proving to be more profitable politically. In this strategy, the making of communal consciousness acquires *longue durée* significance by the production of communal moments, which leads to communal polarization directly and indirectly.

Certain political parties try to drag out these small clashes or communal moments and arouse and sustain a communal consciousness in both the communities involved. They also want to inculcate fear and suspicion within their target oppressed group or the opposing group. This accumulation of fear gets converted into an aggressive vicious circle at the time of elections, in the name of saving their 'honour' or to avenge 'humiliation' at the hands of the other community. Big riots need long-term preparation to create communal moments, such as collecting arms and ammunition, piling up multiple tensions between communities, and so on. In this pyramid of tensions, the immediate triggers, such as playing religious messages or songs on a loudspeaker or throwing stones at a mob, mosque or temple may erupt into bigger violence. However, for small clashes there is no need for long-term preparation or to wait for or engineer the development of a pyramid of tensions.[6] Due to the continuing fear and tension, the communities may erupt over any immediate minor issue, fuelled by political forces to reap electoral fruit.

When these clashes are covered in the electronic media and newspapers, their mobilizational impact multiplies and influences both the conflicting communities, sometimes across the region and state, which is further aggravated by an alert and active communal consciousness among the people. Thus the impact of small clashes is no less than big riots, but the political groups inciting them are not subjected to as much criticism as for big riots.[7] This phenomenon is more suitable for political forces to harness votes based on religious identity. A cadre of a local religion-based organization told me during an interview in 2013, *'Agar kam mehnat, loss and investment me zyaada fayda ho raha ho toh kyon bada risk lein?'* (If there is more profit with less effort, loss and investment, why should we take a bigger risk?) This does not mean that these small communal clashes are free from the possibility of turning into big communal riots, but in the absence of long-term preparation, it becomes more difficult to transform them. The earlier large-scale riots used to lose their effect after a few days, due to the long intervals. But small communal clashes have a greater effect in terms of persisting tension. According to an investigation by the *Indian Express*, police records show that over 600 'communal incidents' or small religious conflicts took place in UP since the Lok Sabha results in 2014. The largest number of communal clashes took place in western UP, i.e., 259. In the Terai region, 29 clashes took place, in the Awadh region there were 53 riots, in Bundelkhand there were 6 riots, while in eastern UP there were 16 riots. A further analysis of the statistics by the *Express* team showed that the regions where most of the communal riots took place were around those where the Assembly by-polls were held soon after the general elections.[8]

If we deeply analyse the data provided by the *Indian Express* we find that more clashes took place in western UP where the by-polls were held in five constituencies; whereas in the regions where the by-polls were held in less number of constituencies, the clashes too were fewer. However, the comparative proportion of riots was much higher in western UP than in the other regions. Usually, the socio-economic-political ground of the region has to be conducive for such clashes to occur. Western UP is the most developed region of UP, which had reaped the maximum benefits of the Green Revolution and came to be known as Harit (Green) Pradesh.[9] However, the benefits of the Green Revolution did not spread evenly but remained confined to a few castes. This region is steeped in feudalism and the prosperity widened the gap between the different castes and communities. The jealousy and anxiety spawned from the uneven development further intensified the feudal pride that already existed in this region. There is a prevailing perception that the socio-economic gap between the Hindu Jats and the Muslim Jats significantly increased after the revolution. The percentage of population of Muslims in this region is also the highest in the entire state of UP. There is no parliamentary constituency here where the population of Muslims is less than 20 to 25 per cent, and in some constituencies it is above 40 per cent.[10] In this situation, Muslims are not a passive community but are highly active and aspiring, and are trying hard to increase their space and visibility in the development process.

Analysing the nature of the small clashes that took place in western UP, we can see that most of them were conflicts to establish dominance over other communities. Several of them were over trivial issues, as noted earlier. As many as 120 of the 600-odd communal incidents were triggered by the use of loudspeakers in masjids and temples.[11] Although loudspeakers are not always used during religious festivals, slowly members of all religions started using them to assert their identity and the 'dominance of visibility'. The use of loudspeakers by both communities shows a greater tendency towards spreading anarchy and hurting the feelings of other communities rather than to assert their freedom. Other trivial reasons for communal incidents were arguments over who should be served first in a local eatery, the use of public conveniences by one community, the grazing of cattle by a member of one community in a field owned by a member of another community, the cutting of a neem tree, small collisions between children riding bicycles and minor motorbike accidents, bathing in ponds and canals, and so on.[12]

Due to this combination of political and economic reasons, communal conflicts in north India have been slowly making inroads into villages whereas earlier they were mainly an urban phenomenon.[13] Various news agencies have reported the growing activities of the RSS in western UP.[14] The presence of the RSS with its affiliates provides aggressive confidence to the dominant Hindu communities in this region to respond to pressures of certain dominant forces in Muslim communities who sometimes also work to instigate them. But, as the RSS was not interested in escalating the small clashes between the people of the two communities, its cadres did not flare up the tension to transform these into larger conflicts. At the same time, the RSS uses the impact after the clash to strengthen Hindutva ideology.

Political Advantage

The spread of trade and commerce in western UP played an important role in the significant expansion of the different branches of the RSS, which was trying to increase the cultural assertion of Hindutva. Immediately after Independence, the Arya Samaj was very active in western UP and had played a progressive role among the Hindus there. It was the trading and merchant communities who formed the main base social groups of the Arya Samaj. But when the Arya Samaj consciousness declined, it was submerged within Hindutva consciousness. The members of the Sangh Parivar do not have any dilemma about creating polarization based on religious identity through the spread of their concept of Hindutva. The BJP, an RSS inspired political agency,[15] has been working on linking the desire for development with the creation of a 'Maha Hindu' identity, by creating a political condition based on religious identity, and has reaped great benefit from it. For the SP, BSP and Congress, communal riots are now a lost game, because the polarization of Hindus cut their Hindu base and marginalized them. Thus, all the three parties try to obtain a share of the remaining smaller vote bank, mainly Muslims. All the three parties are thus compelled to play the politics of religious mobilization. To reply to the BJP's strategies, the SP and Congress both had to take the benefit of Muslim mobilization in UP, but only when there was the possibility of linking the caste vote bank with the Muslim vote bank.

In the new political scenario, with the emergence of a majoritarian mode of politics, when the Yadav base of the SP, the Dalit base of the BSP and the urban and upper-caste votes of the Congress have started moving towards the BJP due to Hindutva mobilization, the consolidation of Muslims is no longer as beneficial for these parties. The umbrella Maha Hindu identity is poised to make the Muslim vote base irrelevant. At the local level, it is possible that in some Assembly elections these three political parties may gain some advantage, but only if their Hindu vote bank is intact and is combined with Muslim votes. Since all the three parties are struggling for a share in the same set of minority Muslim votes, they compete to project themselves as 'protector' of the rights and interests of the Muslim public in UP and also in other parts of India. Due to the Hindutva mobilization, these political parties suffer from political anxiety, because of which their initial political base is under fear of breaking.

The worst situation is that of the BSP, since Hindutva mobilization has pitted the Dalits and Muslims against each other. A ninth of all communal incidents since 16 May 2014 saw the confrontation of Dalits and Muslims.[16] One such incident took place in Katauli Kala of Azamgarh district on 4 August 2014. A minor argument over widening a village road resulted in a violent clash, leaving eight people injured, even though there was no history of tension between the two communities earlier.[17] The Dalit vote of the BSP, which was very strong in western UP, is now under fear of being lost. When the party tries to bring the Muslims under its umbrella, there is a fear of the Dalits separating, and when they support the Dalits, the Muslims appear ready to break away. This was why the party president, Mayawati, has been unable to take much action in this communally fraught situation.[18] As we have seen in the preceding chapters, the use of aggressive religion-based identity politics in regions where Dalits are in a majority is a part of the long-term strategy of the Sangh Parivar to convert and subsume Dalit consciousness within a broader Hindutva consciousness. This may be seen as the formation of 'Hindutva common sense'. Due to various reasons, the Hindu public has started viewing things in its everyday life from the perspective of Hindutva identity. This identity consciousness may be triggered any time and mobilized electorally by just mentioning certain terms of polarization.

During its electoral campaign, the BJP used phrases, such as, 'kabristan–shamshan' and 'Ali–Bajrang Bali' (religious figures of both communities).[19] These religious identity–based terms, used oppositionally, were woven effectively with its development discourse, which worked well during both the 2014 and the 2019 parliamentary elections. During the 2014 election, the BJP used a right-wing strategy that sought to appeal to its Hindu vote base. In a multi-cornered contest, its strategy of focusing on core vote banks was predictable yet interesting—even as it continued to play up the development card. Rajnath Singh, the party president during 2014 parliamentary election, was championing the cause of development while Narendra Modi was mixing up the message on development with a sense of Hindutva.[20] The message of Hindutva was being sought to be communicated through various means. Firstly, the RSS, which had maintained a low profile in the general election of 2009, became active before the 2014 election. After Modi, a former pracharak, was appointed the head of the BJP election committee, Ashok Singhal, leader of the VHP, set up camp at Ayodhya, from where he made every effort to revive the festering Ram Janmabhoomi issue.[21]

Amit Shah, the BJP's face in UP, during the campaign for the 2014 parliamentary election tried to make people believe that Hindutva was a national issue.[22] Not only were pictures of Shah sporting the *tilak-chandan* on his forehead published all over the newspapers in UP, he too had camped in Ayodhya, declaring that Ram Janmabhoomi was a major issue for the 2014 election. The political ramifications were loud and clear. Shah was clearly signalling that the Ayodhya issue was being added to the 'development champion' image of Modi to convert the BJP's campaign into the desired 'development plus' package.

A meeting of seers and sadhus held on 27 June 2013 and chaired by Singhal decided that during the *chauraasi parikrama* (eighty-four circumambulations) of Ayodhya, beginning on 25 August 2013, the issue of Ram Janmabhoomi would be stirred up and given a fresh lease of life.[23]

The second strategy was to bring on board the Hindu sect owing allegiance to the Gorakhnath temple in Gorakhpur, a holy and revered place of the Nath sect. While its leader, Mahant Advaiynath, had been at the forefront of the campaign for the Ram Janmabhoomi, he was known to be a close associate of L.K. Advani's. After Modi's appearance as the face of the BJP for the 2019 elections, this created differences within the larger Hindutva group. Here, Amit Shah emerged as a unifying factor in UP. Shah led the efforts to manage a compromise, and as part of this strategy, he spent many hours with the mahant to appease and assure him of his significance to Modi's camp. Shah succeeded in dissolving the internal division, which made the Hindutva movement much more potent.[24]

Third, efforts were on to engage in youth outreach to tap into their aspirations. In UP, the RSS tried to spread shakhas in parks, hostels and villages, with young people in their twenties and thirties being associated with it. The RSS had decided that in every district it would start forty new shakhas.[25] Alongside, taking the cue from the RSS chief Mohan Bhagwat, the search was on for a *nayak* (hero or icon) in each village in UP.

Finally, keeping Modi in mind as the face of the 2014 parliamentary election, the BJP also used the backward-caste card. The party played this up during the campaign, asserting that even Sardar Patel was from a backward caste. The Gujarat government declared that it would erect the world's tallest statue dedicated to Patel, and work on it started in late 2013. Calling it the Statue of Unity helped them to attract many OBC communities towards the party. The BJP also embarked on a plan to get farmers in villages to donate old farming implements made of iron—as a tribute to Patel, who was often referred to as the *lohpurush*, or Iron Man.

In 2014, the BJP moved towards the agenda of development and started linking it with Hindutva identity. An environment of polarization is always present at places where Muslims are there in impressive numbers along with Hindus, and they play a decisive role in the elections. The BJP was clearly looking to exploit this tension in UP at that time; small skirmishes inspired by Muslim fringe groups were used to claim that Hindus were being victimized under the rule of the SP.[26]

The small clash phenomenon worked well for exacerbating polarization for both the BJP and the non–BJP kind of political forces. From 2014 onwards, until the BJP came to power in the UP Assembly in 2017, a few incidents of small clashes kept occurring that tensed up the environment. These helped in forming a broader Hindu social mobilization in favour of the BJP. After 2017, the polarizational acts by Hindutva forces reduced in number.

In the forty years since 1980, Hindutva consciousness slowly crept into the social structure of the Hindu population and has now finally entered their mindset. So, Hindutva forces no longer need obvious inflammatory tactics to garner political support. During 2019 in UP there were no major polarizational acts by Hindutva forces because they did not require them. In fact, 'thinking as Hindu' or formation of the Hindutva identity has evolved at the level of the Hindu middle class. They now need a mere hint, an evocative statement, an identity-sensitive phrase to move in support of Hindutva politics because of the constant work of Hindutva organizations all these years.

It is interesting to note that after 2017, although the small clashes were not very recurrent, the cases of mob lynching, which had reared their head as a phenomenon with an incident in 2015 in Dadri, UP, rose in various Hindi-speaking states.[27] Interestingly, the RSS saw these incidents as anti-Sangh and anti-Hindutva by small local organizations, which may or may not have been influenced by the RSS-based Hindutva discourse. But now that the BJP was in power, the political ambitions of such fringe elements had emerged at a level that they wanted to acquire prominence and importance by committing such acts. In most of the mob lynching cases, one may find the involvement of such fringe elements who claimed themselves to be 'protectors' of Hindu religion. One RSS pracharak told me in a discussion that they had trouble controlling such elements and balance the situation, so that such incidents did not grow in the future. He further said: *'Yeh vichitra sthiti hai, humne unhe Shiv ki tarah aashirvad bhi nahi diya aur woh humein Bhasmasur ki tarah jala rahe hain.'* (It is a strange situation. We have not blessed them the way Shiva had blessed Bhasmasur, yet they are burning us.) So the RSS is facing the dilemma of how to rein in the burgeoning negative impact of religious identity–based mobilization as the RSS, according to its public assertions, aspires to form a society with balance that does not clash and conflict. The Delhi Riots of 2020 raise questions on some of these observations. But I would like to propose that the polarization psyche may or may not be converted into full-fledged communal riots. The mainstream Hindutva political and social groups want to use polarization for limited purposes. However, certain fringe elements claiming to be Hindutva organizations try to misuse the conditions prepared by the strategy of polarization, which may be seen as a spillover effect. It can be used by both the Hindutva and non-Hindutva fringe elements simultaneously.

4

THE RSS IN ELECTIONS

Political and Apolitical

'People who understand everything get no stories'

—Bertolt Brecht[1]

In this chapter we will try to understand the role of the RSS cadres in building up the 2014 parliamentary election campaign in favour of the BJP and reshaping the electoral image of Narendra Modi. It is based on primary research comprising field visits to UP and on newspaper reports. During the course of the 2014 Lok Sabha election campaign there had been a tremendous image building of the then Gujarat chief minister and the BJP's 'prime ministerial nominee', Narendra Modi, in the media. The entire campaigning was known to have been done by the BJP, which was handling his brand-building, highlighting issues, the agenda of the party and the electioneering. In most of the analyses, the credit for Modi's successful campaign was being given to corporate public relations agencies and youth adherents, particularly those who are proficient in using information technology tools.[2] What was less known, however, was the role of the RSS in providing perspective and structure to the entire campaign. The BJP is the political wing of the RSS, and the RSS claims that it would never work for a political party. But since the candidature of Narendra Modi was announced, a significant section of RSS cadres took over a large part of the organizational activities of electing and promoting Narendra Modi into their own hands. This is despite the statement by Mohan Bhagwat, the RSS chief, in Bengaluru (formerly Bangalore), that projecting Narendra Modi was not their agenda.[3] In Bhagwat's opinion, 'their agenda is to bring issues in front of the people. Since the RSS is not a political party we have our own limitations.'[4]

Election Campaigning by RSS Cadres

In spite of the suggestion of their sarsanghchalak, in the final phases of the elections of 2014, the RSS cadres were completely focused on promoting the image of Modi. Although the advertising and publicity for Modi were being powered by a campaign visible in the media that reached out mainly to the urban population, on the ground, particularly in UP, it was being monitored by RSS cadres. Reports in various newspapers indicate that nearly one lakh RSS group leaders and six lakh cadres from 42,000 units spread across the country[5] were working full-time to ensure the BJP's victory. A high-level team of Sangh leaders had set up a control room in Varanasi from where it kept an eye on all the party workers round the clock. The team was being led by

Amit Shah, Narendra Modi's right-hand man, assisted by Sunil Bansal, a top RSS-trained organizer and leader.

One of the methods adopted by RSS cadres was to visit remote villages using carriages named 'NaMo Rath'. According to reports, nearly 400 such carriages had been gathered and they had been used (or at least targeted) to reach a majority of the villages in UP, Uttarakhand and Himachal Pradesh.[6] These carriages were inscribed with large portraits of Narendra Modi and they went about campaigning with loud advertisement jingles promoting him. The carriages halted at road crossings and village chaupals screening campaign-related films and entertaining crowds. RSS volunteers had also fanned out to many villages for aggressive door-to-door campaigning.

The RSS as a Feedback Forum

The headquarters of the RSS in Prayagraj is situated near Tashkent Marg, adjacent to the

Jwala Devi School. It is called Ananda Ashram and, in the run-up to the 2014 general election, it became a focus of attention. A sprinkling of leaders of the BJP could be seen in its office and, similarly, the BJP office had some RSS leaders present. The situation in Varanasi, headquarters of the Kashi Mandal, and Lucknow, were no different. This narrative captures the altered circumstances well.

The RSS, which is a right-wing voluntary Hindu organization, has conventionally cultivated the image of an institution that pursues the social and cultural revival of Hinduism. As far as the BJP was concerned, it was always a force behind the scenes, never in the forefront. However, as the 2014 parliamentary elections came closer, the relationship between the RSS and the BJP altered significantly, with the RSS influence on the BJP becoming more overt. Part of the reason might have been the fading away of the older generation of leaders such as Atal Bihari Vajpayee and L.K. Advani, who, with their strong personalities, were intimidating to the RSS. But, ever since leaders such as Nitin Gadkari and Rajnath Singh, with a considerable smaller political base, gained prominence, the RSS began to assert itself. This was visible at the BJP conclave in Goa in the manner in which the RSS swayed the debate over the appointment of Narendra Modi, an RSS member, as chairperson of the BJP's election committee.[7] The RSS also convened a meeting in New Delhi in which Suresh (Bhaiyyaji) Joshi, Suresh Soni and Dattatreya Hasabale represented the RSS, while from the BJP the leaders Rajnath Singh, Sushma Swaraj and Arun Jaitley were in attendance. In this meeting, the RSS declared Modi as the prime ministerial candidate. The impact was immediate. Modi emerged as the BJP's new poster boy, replacing Advani, around the slogan: *Naya Nara, Nayi Soch aur Nayi Ummeed* (new slogan, new thinking and new hope).[8]

In July 2013, the RSS had conducted a meeting of its *pranthpracharak*s (regional volunteers) at Amravati, Maharashtra, and instructed them to ensure coordination between the RSS cadres and the BJP in the next general election. The local RSS cadres worked at various places as facilitators to rally the entire Sangh Parivar for the general election of 2014 and also leverage low-intensity polarization[9] and consolidate the Hindu vote, like it did in the mid-1990s around Ayodhya. Clearly, the RSS was no longer the non-playing captain and their hard work and relentless effort was paying off.

Apart from helping the BJP in the electioneering process, the RSS also worked as a mediator to resolve thorny issues within the BJP. Just after this political event, at Nagpur, the RSS leadership called Advani, Murli Manohar Joshi and Rajnath Singh individually to help ease and iron out all controversies emanating from the party's leadership issues.

The RSS has a network of organizations. The BJP is the RSS's inspired political organization. The VHP is the organization spreading the Hindutva political agenda around emotive religious issues. The Bajrang Dal is a ground-level youth organization. The Vanvasi Kalyan Ashram is engaged in promoting Hindu norms among tribals. And the Rashtriya Sevika Samiti is its women's wing. In addition, the Sangh Parivar includes other organizations such as the Saraswati Shishu Mandir schools, which seek to indoctrinate youth with a 'saffron' interpretation of social and cultural issues.

The RSS was also engaged in collecting feedback on the impact of Narendra Modi's speeches during his electoral rallies prior to the 2014 elections. In November 2013, I visited Bahraich with a research team to study a rally organized by the BJP and addressed by Narendra Modi. As the rally ended, we noticed a group of around fifty people taking feedback from the audience about Modi's speech in their local language. They were asking questions such as 'How did you like Modiji's speech? What is your opinion on what he said about armed Muslims? He has also challenged the dominant Muslim groups of this region. What is your opinion about it?' Through these and several such related questions they were trying to obtain feedback from different people. Some of them had recording devices in their hands while some were just interacting orally. Their aim appeared to be to understand the reaction of Hindus to the assertive speech challenging violent Muslim groups, besides seeking their opinion on Modi's plans for development. The speech was given just a few days after the bomb blast that took place during his Patna rally.[10]

We could ascertain that the volunteers collecting information had something to do with the RSS as they later went to the RSS office in Bahraich. Something similar happened after Modi's rally in Raja Talab in Varanasi in December 2013. Here, too, an organized group of people was found to be collecting responses from the people who had stayed behind at a gathering at a crossing a little way off. Later the volunteers moved together to the RSS office. Here, their chief objective seemed to have been to collect informal opinions of common people on Modi's speech about the cleaning of the Ganga at Varanasi, his criticisms of Congress leader Rahul Gandhi, and his slogan of working towards a 'Congress-free India'. They were also seen to be interacting with potential voters at tea stalls who had not necessarily come to the rally.

We tried to find out more about the activities of the RSS volunteers at both these rallies from a local volunteer. The man, speaking to us on the promise of anonymity, told us that a group of RSS volunteers collect information about the impact of the main issues of Modi's speech from the listeners at the rally. When we asked him what was done with the information he was not very forthcoming, but after some prodding he told us that it was presented at rally review meetings held at the local RSS offices. The main issues that emerged from the responses of the common people were then presented at the RSS shakhas held in big cities and towns. This feedback was then taken to the top brass of the RSS.

If we believe this volunteer, it appears that through these shakhas, Narendra Modi's image was being recreated and disseminated to the voters. Alongside, insights were being gathered for Modi's future speeches and the mobilizational strategies of the BJP were then chalked out. In the context of the 2014 elections, Modi's speeches are considered the most influential and effective mobilizational tool of the BJP, which was based on organizing his rallies and then gauging the impact of his speeches by the RSS.

In this manner the RSS not only spreads messages about the Hindutva ideology among the common people but also takes input from them. This information is first given to the Sangh and then to the BJP, which forms the basis for ongoing electoral strategies of the party. This was observed in both the 2014 and 2019 elections.

RSS Cadres and Booth Management

Another important activity of a section of the RSS cadres was polling-booth management and both the RSS and the BJP had formed booth management committees at the ground level across villages and small towns in UP both during the 2014 and 2019 elections. While the BJP had formed twenty-five-member teams for each booth, whose task was to interact with the voters of their particular booths, RSS cadres too had formed parallel booth committees in each constituency. The committees comprised ten to twenty highly empowered volunteers depending on the place and its situation. For example, if a place is dominated by Dalits and backward castes, the committee members were selected from within these communities.

In order to reach out to women, RSS cadres trained women leaders and supporters of the BJP with whom they were constantly in touch. The committee members identified the temperament and thinking of each household in their constituency, and each day the members met some of the households and tried to gauge their thinking. If any household was found to be dissatisfied with Modi's persona or the politics he represented, they gently tried to convince all the family members about the positive aspects of Modi's rule and his leadership. The most important task of the committee members was to ensure that the people to whom this outreach was extended were taken to vote in the respective booths on election days. The organizing team of the RSS that was supervising Narendra Modi's electioneering had adopted a very strict attitude and the volunteers who failed to bring the selected families in and around the booth were held accountable.

In addition to the RSS team, a team of highly skilled professionals had spread out across the districts and cities of UP during both the elections, with the mission of keeping a watch on the local teams working in each district to campaign for Modi and to report directly to Amit Shah. The trademark dress code of this team was blue kurta and blue jeans, and they were known as the 'blue brigade'.[11] The members of this team were part of the CAG, and most of them were graduates in professional courses from reputed colleges and universities both in India and the United States. Using technological tools and know-how, this set of technical professionals masterminded various aspects of campaigns such as the '*Chai pe Charcha*' ('conversations over tea', either in physical locations or in Internet chats), Modi 3D rallies (featuring holographic technology enabling 'simulcasting' of Narendra Modi's rallies), and so on.[12] This team was divided into two-member units which were sent to each Lok Sabha constituency. These units were entrusted with the task of judging the activities of the local teams and where the local team was not very efficient, the members of the technical team themselves formed the campaign teams. The technical team members regularly updated the central unit of Modi's team about their activities.

According to the BJP leaders, the technical team had looked after several election campaigns, such as the 2007 UP Assembly elections. The team functioned independently of the district and city committees but it was in touch with all the candidates of the BJP.

The team members spread out across the constituencies of UP also had a list of names and telephone numbers of the officers of the BJP's booth management committees.[13] The team had also asked for the formation of groups of ten local workers in all these constituencies who were devoted in their duty of campaigning for the BJP. These workers were made members of the existing booth committees and it is reported the technical team had changed nearly two dozen booth committees in consultation with the district party organization. Effectively, they had formed their own booth committees parallel to the booth committees of the RSS and the BJP. The technical team monitored the needs of the local candidates and the input was sent to the central team, which provided the necessary support to the local BJP candidates. This team also worked in coordination with the RSS team and they exchanged information and inputs to form strategies for electoral mobilization. In the final phase of the 2014 elections, various arms of the Sangh Parivar, the RSS itself, the

BJP cadres and a team of technically equipped workers, 'the blue brigade', worked round the clock for the success of Narendra Modi's personality-oriented campaign.

5

POLITICS, NARRATIVES
AND ELECTIONS

Jis rajneeti ke pas mithak aur dantkathaye hoti hain,
woh hi shaktiwaan hoti hai.

—Ram Dhiraj, a social activist

(The politics that possess myths and mythical
stories ultimately becomes powerful.)

Politics is all about framing narratives. Political
parties have traditionally used a variety of
propaganda strategies and media management
tricks, besides manifestos and rallies, to frame
their narratives. The social bases of these
narrative formations may be derived from caste,
religion, ethnic identity, national security and
various other issues that mobilize communities

133

in favour of political parties. Political analysts believe that such narratives play an important role in shaping electoral fortunes. Here I would like to see how the BJP and the other members of the Hindutva family formed their politics during the recent democratic elections, especially in UP, where it won the Assembly elections in 2017 and how other political parties explored the resource base for their own narratives. In this chapter, we have evolved our discourses based on the context of the parliamentary elections of 2014 and 2019, and the 2017 UP state Assembly election.

War of Narratives

For the 2019 elections the BJP tried to frame the conversation around national security issues, especially the strike on 26 February on a terrorist training camp in Balakot, Pakistan. Issues related to the terrorist attack in Pulwama on 14 February 2019 played an important role in making people generally receptive to the subject of national security. In times when insecurity has sway over the social psyche, such narratives provide a sense of confidence. Promises for security may, therefore, attract a section of the Indian public and voters.

In contrast, development, which was the BJP-led NDA's main plank in the 2014 election, became a sub-narrative in the 2019 elections. In response to the ruling party's efforts, the Congress, under Rahul Gandhi, came up with the Nyay-based narrative; Nyay, meaning justice, is an abbreviated form for Nyuntam Aay Yojana, or minimum wage programme. The Congress criticized the policies of the Narendra Modi–led government for causing unemployment and failing to tackle rural distress. It also made several promises to address these problems and promised to launch the Nyay scheme if it came to power. The Nyay scheme was based on hard economic and social realities, while the BJP's narrative of national security was based on emotive issues centred on nationalism and national identity.

In contrast to the two major national parties, i.e., the BJP and the Congress, over the years, the All India Anna Dravida Munnetra Kazhagam (AIADMK), Trinamool Congress, Telugu Desam Party, Telangana Rashtriya Samiti and other regional political parties that were not built around the politics of affirmative action have developed state-centric narratives. The narrative of caste has not been pushed by either the national or the regional parties, but it has nevertheless influenced the formation of caste-based and social alliances by political parties. The caste narrative, though present, has hitherto been overshadowed or assimilated by the Hindutva narrative, which has been trying to include it under its broader argument. Eventually, the caste narrative emerged as an important trope in the 2019 election. The SP–BSP alliance, through rallies and various propaganda techniques, strongly asserted and pushed caste as an important electoral issue in its zones of influence.

In her election speech in Mainpuri on 19 April 2019, Mayawati talked about Mulayam Singh Yadav as the 'real OBC' (*pichhda* or backward) and Narendra Modi as a 'fake OBC' and '*kagzipichhda*' (backward only on paper).[1] The SP–BSP alliance was based on the coming together of two caste-based social groups, i.e., OBCs and Dalits. In his speeches and tweets, Akhilesh Yadav tried to use caste as a mobilizational tactic to counter the BJP's nationalism-based narrative. His remarks like '*doodhwala* versus *chaiwala*' (milkman vs tea seller)[2] were targeted at the Yadavs who are milkmen by caste and profession. Akhilesh also talked of Dalit–Pichhda unity, together called 'Bahujan'. This strategy aimed to turn the battle of 2019 as one between the Dalit–OBC combine and the BJP's Hindutva and hyper-nationalism.

As we know, UP Chief Minister Yogi Adityanath, one of the BJP's star campaigners, tried to set the narrative of communal mobilization through his statements on Ali and Bajrang Bali.[3] Later, Mayawati turned the UP chief minister's slogan on its head by arguing that Bajrang Bali belongs to the Dalit and vanchit community. Ali and Bajrang Bali both are ours, she said.[4]

Similarly, in Bihar, *aarakshan* (reservation) became a powerful plank for RJD leader Tejashwi Yadav. Yadav had been reminding OBCs and Dalits of the value of reservation, while warning them that the BJP could take away this important instrument of empowerment if it came to power. In some of his speeches and tweets, Tejashwi positioned reservation as an important tool available to the underprivileged. He also coined slogans like 'Jai Arakshan' and tried to reignite the memory of the Mandal Commission report, positioning it against the Hindutva rhetoric.

Regional parties in south India put the BJP on the defensive for using the Hindutva narrative as its main poll plank. Even so, while national security, with the development claim as the subplot, was the BJP's main narrative, the party had not left the caste question untouched. It was also forming social alliances at the grassroots with various caste-based political parties in the north and regional parties in the south. A case in point is the Janata Dal (United), or JD(U), in Bihar. The Yadavs,

Koiris and Kurmis are the major caste groups among the OBCs in that state. The Yadavs were with the RJD, but the other two were with the JD(U). Nitish Kumar of the JD(U) expanded his voter base by adding MBCs and 'Mahadalits' to his target constituencies. During the elections, Nitish and the BJP both benefited from their alliance.[5]

'Samagra Hindutva'

A strategy framed by the BJP for the 2019 election was the formation of 'Samagra Hindutva' (Integrated Hindutva). The BJP government in UP organized a 'Samrasta Kumbh' (United Kumbh) in Ayodhya on 15 December 2018, whose main purpose was to invite Dalits and other marginalized communities into the Hindutva fold. While inaugurating the Kumbh, UP Chief Minister Yogi Adityanath opined that most of the Vedic *richa*s (hymns) were composed by Dalit rishis, so stopping Dalits from reading the Vedas is unjust. At a coordination meeting of the BJP and the RSS held on 25 October 2018 in Lucknow, the BJP president Amit Shah said that 'Samagra Hindutva' is an important instrument to counter the Mahagathbandhan, which was a coalition of several political parties of north India, formed in 2019 to oppose the BJP in the electoral battle.[6] This concept was accepted by some RSS activists too who said that it seemed like a novel notion. One of them said: 'In the RSS, we talk about *samagra gram vikas* (collective village development), *samagra samaj* (collective society) but not samagra Hindutva. Instead, we use *ekatmmanavvad* as propounded by the late Deendayal Upadhyay to denote the oneness of entire humanity.'[7]

The RSS and Sangh Parivar also talk about uniting Hindu society, but in order to include the Muslims in their narrative they claim that Muslims are those Hindus who converted during the medieval period under the compulsion of Muslim rulers. Thus they should now (re)unite with the Hindus in Hindu society. While explaining 'Samagra Hindutva', Shah suggested that the BJP should integrate

OBC and Dalits in the Hindutva fold as well. He emphasized that the government was working to integrate these communities, and that there was a need to continue a dialogue to integrate them. So, he proposed the formation of a social alliance of SCs, OBCs and castes of the general category under the influence of the BJP. Thus, Shah envisioned a grand *social* alliance to counter a similar political alliance under the Mahagathbandhan. Numerically and politically, this 'saffron' SC–OBC–general caste alliance might have been heavier than the OBC–SC tie-up proposed by Akhilesh Yadav and Mayawati. Therefore, while 'unite all Hindus' has always been the RSS's agenda, politically too, the BJP needed a consolidated Hindu backing to defeat the Mahagathbandhan in UP in 2019.

To go about it, the party tried to take credit for reinforcing the SC/ST Atrocities Act during campaigning in SC/ST-dominated areas.[8] The Central government took the credit for extending the Ujjwala Yojana (free distribution of gas connection) to the OBCs also; it was earlier only available to SC/STs. Thus, the BJP government strategically and systematically started wooing SCs, STs and OBCs towards the party before and after the 2019 elections. In one of the coordination meetings, Shah reportedly told the BJP and the RSS members that 'our government is already working to create "Samagra Hindutva", and the party too should work on that line'.[9] For this, he suggested that party workers should keep interacting with these communities and explain to them the programmes and policies that the government had designed for them.

Apart from policy-level initiatives, as we have described in detail in earlier chapters, the BJP was planning to build Ambedkar memorials in Delhi and London, and an Ambedkar centre in Delhi, to integrate Dalits into the Hindutva fold. Celebrating Dalit heroes like Suheldeo and Daldeo Pasi was another step in the same direction. Even the RSS started keeping pictures of Ambedkar in many of its programmes. One can now find Ambedkar photographs in various RSS offices.

All these strategies were planned efforts to change the BJP's image of a *savarna*-led (upper-caste) party to a party in which SC, ST and OBC communities and castes featured prominently. 'Hindutva' as a term is supposed to include all Hindus. But the addition of the prefix 'Samagra' was a conscious broadening of the BJP's avowed philosophy.

The Kumbh Mela held in 2019 in Prayagraj was another platform for the BJP to evolve this concept. UP's BJP-led government worked closely with the Modi–led Central government to systematically use the symbol of the Kumbh for its samrasta campaign and to create 'Samagra Hindutva', since the Kumbh Mela is attended by lakhs of Hindus of all castes and communities from all over India. Just before this large Kumbh mela, the government organized five smaller Kumbhs at various places in the state with names such as Sanskriti (Cultural) Kumbh, Vichar (Ideology) Kumbh and Samrasta (Harmonious) Kumbh, which were essentially attempts to disseminate Hindutva ideology.[10]

The UP government made a wide array of efforts to showcase the Kumbh, both within and outside the country. It branded the Ardh Kumbh (the half Kumbh, which is held after six years) as a Purna Kumbh (full Kumbh, which is held after twelve years). The UP government changed the nomenclature to make it an impressive brand to attract people. Three major reasons it used this cultural opportunity are: One, to attract a lot more people to the mela. Two, the Kumbh message would at least reach those who could not make it to the mela. Three, creating a grand Hindutva identity by state-supported mega celebrations of Hindu festivals and rituals.

In fact, Yogi Adityanath wrote invitation letters to all pradhans of the state and the country to invite them for the 'Divya and Bhavya Kumbh' (divine and blessed Kumbh), the tagline for this festival.[11] The RSS and its allied organizations tried hard to disseminate Hindutva consciousness by using the Prayag Kumbh as a platform for their various programmes. Various mobilizational meetings of pracharaks were organized by the RSS and its associated organizations such as the VHP and Sanskar Bharati, to reach out to the Hindu public. For instance, Sanskar Bharati organized a nationwide programme around the symbol of the Kumbh. They also organized public meetings and hosted cultural performances near the tributaries of the Ganga. These may be read as attempts by the Sangh Parivar to create opportunities of interaction with the people about Hindutva, and to spread the ideology. Prime Minister Narendra Modi also visited Prayagraj and addressed a rally before the Kumbh Mela officially started in January 2019. He performed several pujas with sants and sadhus and visited the sacred Akshayvat tree in Allahabad Fort.

This visit by Modi may be analysed in two ways. First, it helped in the preparation of the Kumbh and strengthened its symbolism. Second, it may also be read as an effort by the BJP to appropriate the symbolic capital that is a part of such religious festivals. For the BJP government in UP, the Kumbh also worked as an opportunity to showcase its skill at good governance by organizing such a large festival. It appeared as a golden opportunity for Hindutva cultural and political groups to weave and strengthen Hindu identity that the BJP cashed in on successfully during the 2019 parliamentary election.

Caste and Election 2019

All the political parties in the fray in the 2019 elections tried to acquire their 'base votes', that is, the votes of certain dominant and numerically strong castes that a particular party depends upon. Contrary to popular understanding, this may include upper-caste votes, since in Indian democracy, caste hegemony has become strategic. The parties invented new methods of mobilizing and polarizing the various castes. One strategy was exploring the possibility of 'stepney' or 'spare tyre' caste votes. 'Stepney' caste votes are those that do not form the base vote and are numerically less; they get added to the base caste vote to support them.

To cultivate different castes as stepney votes, political parties tried to enter into alliances with these castes.

Another strategy to garner stepney votes was to form alliances with different caste-based parties. In UP, many castes with a certain numerical strength have formed their small caste-based political parties, with which big political parties like the BJP and the SP form alliances. For instance, the BJP formed an alliance with Apna Dal (considered a party of the Kurmis) and the Bharatiya Samaj Party (considered a party of the Rajbhars), while the SP formed an alliance with the Rashtriya Lok Dal (or RLD, considered a party of the Jats). The end result of these strategies is that numerically strong castes get representation according to their strength not only in the elections, but also in different decision-making bodies. On the other hand, the numerically weaker castes (the 'stepney' votes) do not get proper representation; even what little they do sometimes get, is superficial. This informal caste-based distribution of power turns our electoral democracy into a 'castocracy' (*jati-tantra*).

In the 2019 elections, the BJP's caste mobilizational strategy was to focus on the non-Jatav Dalit and non-Yadav backward-caste votes. We saw in chapter 2 that the RSS has been mobilizing these castes through its grassroots work. Under the umbrella identity of 'Hindu', these castes would act as their stepney vote to link them with the upper-caste base votes of the BJP. This would also help in mitigating the challenge these castes pose for the upper castes. For this purpose, it targeted backward castes like Patel, Maurya, Murav, Nishad, Lodh, Kachi and Dalit castes like Pasi, Nai, Dhobhi, Valmiki, Sonkar, Khatik. A parallel strategy of the party was glorifying its influential savarna leaders to keep its base votes intact. To appease it savarna base the BJP tried to create a balance by offering them representation at the organizational level, and showcased its commitment towards the Hindutva agenda by rallying for the construction of the Ram temple in Ayodhya.

Following in the footsteps of the BSP, the BJP also worked on various strategies to satisfy the aspirations of backward and Dalit castes like providing organizational representation, organizing caste-based rallies, and, along with the help of the RSS, celebrating festivals in the memory of their heroes and gods, constructing their temples, and so on—thus luring them towards the party. The party also elected Keshav Prasad Maurya as the UP BJP president which made castes like Maurya, Murav and Kachi feel they had a big role in the BJP. In order to lure the Lodh–Nishad votes, plans were made to provide Kalyan Singh and his son Rajbir Singh important roles during the election campaigns.

Amit Shah also held many caste-based rallies in UP before the elections. He addressed the rallies of Maurya and Patel castes at Andawa in Prayagraj on 22 June 2016. Another rally was organized at the time of the BJP national executive meeting at Prayagraj, in which Prime Minister Narendra Modi mentioned Nishad Raj (deity of Nishad community) at least three times in order to appease the Nishad, Mallah,

Kewat communities.[12] Through these efforts the BJP tried to play the role of highlighting the identity and generating the self-esteem of the OBCs and the Dalits who had not yet received political space. The BJP, for the first time, ensured reservations in posts in the various committees set up by the party from the booth level to the state level and assigned responsibilities to Dalits, backward castes and women.

Parallel to the BJP, the BSP also tried to sharpen its caste politics but in a different way before the 2019 elections. Its endeavour was to strengthen the Dalit–Brahmin concord through its social engineering, in order to associate various other castes with its Dalit base votes, as well as to strengthen the Dalit–Muslim alliance. Mayawati's first step in this direction was to control the dissatisfaction and displeasure that had emerged among the Brahmins in the past. To instil the feelings of brotherhood in the Brahmins she planned a strategy of providing tickets to the Brahmins in large numbers in the 2019 elections. She also tried to prevent

Dalit and backward-castes leaders from passing comments, criticizing and talking aggressively about Brahminical rites and rituals. Mayawati wanted the Brahmins to feel at ease in her party and go along with her. In the past, she had walked on the lines of *Bahujan hitaye, Bahujan sukhaye* (Bahujan welfare, Bahujan joy) and this time she implemented the policy of *Sarvajan hitaye, Sarvajan sukahye* (everyone's welfare, everyone's joy). Although Mayawati provided representation to all the castes from the booth-level to the state-level committees, she kept in mind that the Dalit and OBC representation was not squeezed. However, this time BSP did not hold large *bhaichara* (brotherhood) and *atma samman* (self-respect) rallies of the various castes across constituencies as it had been doing in the past.

During the 2019 elections, the BSP's strategy was not to attract castes by making alliances with small caste-based political parties, pejoratively referred to as *bichauliya* (who sell their own caste votes to another political party), but instead make direct alliances with those castes. It did this by providing self-respect and identity to all the castes and communities as a whole. They provided respect to the icons and heroes of these castes through audiovisual and oral presentations, constructing statues, celebrating their anniversaries, renaming public places and institutions in their memory, and so on. They also offered political representation to the caste and community leaders within the party. Alongside, Mayawati also worked on the strategy of keeping her Dalit base votes intact. In a grand meeting held in Lucknow in 2016, Mayawati warned the party leaders, workers and electoral candidates that they should not think that all Dalit votes will walk to them in the name of Mayawati. For winning the Dalit votes they had to visit Dalit hamlets and ask for their votes. She also warned that the tickets of those candidates who did not follow her instructions would be cancelled. Another strategy to consolidate the Dalit votes was to make her Dalit bhaichara campaigns more active and influential in the reserved constituencies and dissolving the Bhaichara Samitis in other general electoral constituencies. This was done in order to attract other lower and backward-caste voters and link them with her Dalit vote bank to strengthen her base vote.

For the SP, the Yadavs and Muslims had been the base voters in the past but during the 2019 elections one could feel the resentment of the Muslims towards the party.[13] The caste-based mobilization of SP during these elections indicated that on the basis of its Yadav base votes it had planned to assimilate the MBCs within its fold.[14] The party had been giving utmost importance to the MBC votes as a part of its electoral caste arithmetic. To attain this objective, it had been trying to get certain OBC castes classified as SCs since 2005. In 2013, it also pushed for amendments in the UP Public Services (Reservation for Scheduled Castes, Scheduled Tribes and Other Backward Classes) Act, 1994, to get seventeen castes[15] included in the MBC category but did not get a green signal from the Central government.[16] However, this did not deter the SP; even during its last tenure in 2012–17, it constantly raised the demand for the inclusion of certain OBCs in the SC category. In parallel, to satisfy the aggressive Brahmin population at the state level, SP continues to celebrate Parshuram Jayanti and Brahmin Sammelan. Thus, caste again became an important idiom of electoral mobilization in UP during the 2019 elections.

Which Narrative Won

The BJP-led NDA won a mammoth victory in the 2019 parliamentary elections. The BJP won 55 of the 80 Lok Sabha seats in UP, which was in contrast to the reading of political analysts, who had expected the Mahagathbandhan of the SP and BSP to pose a severe challenge to the BJP. The SP–BSP alliance, backed by the SCs and OBCs, was deemed an unassailable social coalition. So what can explain the success of the BJP in UP?

First, the BJP, which has its core vote among the upper castes, who are numerically substantial in UP, went for a strategic micro-management of castes and crafted a new social equation. This too was a 'gathbandhan', albeit of non–Yadav, numerically substantial OBC communities, such as Kurmi, Maurya, etc., and MBCs including Nishads, Bind, Kasera, Kumhar, Thathera and Tamboli. The party also reached out to non-Jatav Dalit castes such as Musahars, Nat, Kanjar and Kuchbadhiya. The BJP built this alliance by organizing caste conferences of various most-backward and non-Jatav Dalit castes while also ensuring that the benefits of schemes like Ujjwala Yojana, Pradhan Mantri Aawas Yojana (urban housing scheme) and the Mudra loan reached them. In this way, it crafted a larger, wider social coalition than the Mahagathbandhan of the SP, BSP and RLD. Feedback from the RSS helped the party to build and manage this coalition. As detailed in earlier chapters, Dalit and MBC caste heroes were reinterpreted by the BJP–RSS leadership as Hindutva warriors to attract their respective communities towards this narrative.

Second, *vote-katua*s (vote cutters) like the Congress and Pragatishil Samajwadi Party of Shivpal Singh Yadav worked against the

Mahagathbandhan. The Congress's tactic was to field candidates who could work as vote-katuas against the BJP in many seats. The tactic misfired as many of the Congress candidates were former members of the SP and the BSP, who had been denied tickets by their own party. They cut into the Mahagathbandhan's votes, which in turn benefited the BJP.

Third, the SP and BSP cadres did not get sufficient time to build a rapport on the ground together as part of the Mahagathbandhan. In our field trips during the 2019 parliamentary election, we could sense the rivalry among the cadres in many constituencies, which, however, was not overt. The interests of the Jatavs and Yadavs worked at cross purposes at the grassroots. This conflict also worked at multiple levels, for instance, between the landholding Yadavs and landless Dalits, and the traditionally socially dominant Yadavs and the newly assertive Jatavs. It also affected the transfer of votes between the parties.

Fourth, there was the emergence of an aspirational class of voters that identified with

Prime Minister Narendra Modi. This situation was similar to 1991 when the economic reforms initiated by the Congress under the prime ministership of P.V. Narasimha Rao had unleashed economic aspirations across age groups, genders and castes. This section of aspiring classes, which has emerged in the present period, connects with the politics of the BJP and is attracted towards its neo-right agendas. Issues such as national security, the call for a strong decisive leadership, the cornering of Pakistan and other such slogans motivated them to support the party. They backed the BJP in 2014, and their loyalty to the BJP was evident in 2019 as well.

Fifth, the Modi government, through policies and programmes, mobilized various marginalized communities *horizontally* to counter the BSP and the SP, which mobilized castes vertically. The SP and the BSP gave space to the visible and dominant castes among the Dalits and mobilized them to rise vertically in the overall socio-economic hierarchy, while the BJP worked for the ignored and invisible communities among the Dalits, to offer them horizontal mobility within the Dalit community. The reservation for economically backward sections among the upper castes— the Economic Weaker Section Reservation Bill was enacted as law with great swiftness in January 2019—simultaneously helped to dilute the dissatisfaction among the upper castes, especially the Brahmins, who perceived UP Chief Minister Yogi Adityanath to be favouring specific castes. It also diluted the upper-caste anger against the BJP's ambivalence on the SC-ST Act, which had played a significant role in the party's defeat in the Assembly elections in Madhya Pradesh, Chhattisgarh and Rajasthan in 2018. This new set of reservations helped the party to assuage the upper castes in northern India, particularly in UP.

The impressive success of the BJP and the failure of Mahagathbandhan in UP may have far-reaching consequences for Indian politics. Political parties may have to redefine the politics of social justice in north India. The relationship between caste and politics may have to be revisited. OBCs and SCs are not homogeneous communities. Their inherent heterogeneity is brought to the fore by competitive democracy and socio-economic aspirations. The BJP has been savvy to the fault lines within these heterogeneities and has accordingly crafted new social and political equations.

6

THE ROAD AHEAD

Framing Own Public

After the uprising of the 17th June
The Secretary of the Writers Union
Had leaflets distributed in the Stalinallee
Stating that the people
Had forfeited the confidence of the government
And could win it back only
By redoubled efforts. Would it not be easier
In that case for the government
To dissolve the people
And elect another?

—Bertolt Brecht[1]

After the amazing victory of the BJP in the 2019 parliamentary election in which it won more than 300 seats by itself, the question arose in the minds of the people as to what this government was going to do in its second term. The Muslim Women (Protection of Rights on Marriage) Bill, floated in 2017, was aimed at ending the practice of Muslim men divorcing their wives by chanting 'talaq' thrice (triple talaq). It was passed as an act by both the houses of Parliament on 30 July 2019.[2] Article 370, which gave special status to Jammu and Kashmir, was modified on 5 August 2019, and Jammu and Kashmir turned into a Union Territory.[3] Ladakh, which was earlier a part of the state of J&K was made a separate Union Territory. The long-running Ram Janmabhoomi dispute reached a settlement after the Supreme Court judgment on 9 November 2019.[4] And the Citizenship (Amendment) Act (CAA), which amended the existing 1955 act, was passed by the Parliament on 11 December 2019.[5] After this, the government intended to implement the National Register of Citizens (NRC) across the country.[6]

All these issues were part of the BJP manifesto before the 2019 elections.[7] After delivering on these, what other issues will the

Narendra Modi–led government influence and what new elements will Modi and his government add to the politics of democracy? What challenges do the Sangh and its family members face and how are they going to resolve them?

Reorganizing Social Groups

One issue which has always created a difficult situation for the RSS and Hindutva politics is the issue of reservation. The RSS is of the view that reservation to the OBCs should be maintained along with the SCs but their pracharaks sometimes feel that it creates a divided society in India.[8] These feelings of the RSS grassroot cadres have been reaching their chief Mohan Bhagwat during the feedback meetings of the Sangh held from time to time. Secondly, RSS cadres have also been reporting that the benefit of the current reservation policies is being cornered by a section of OBC and SC communities. They found that many Dalit castes were feeling deprived from the

162

benefits of reservation policies, and political parties like the BSP and SP were not sensitive towards their desires. The leadership of both political parties are dominated, respectively, by the Yadav and the Jatav castes. All these reports compelled Mohan Bhagwat to suggest a review of the current reservation policy.[9]

The success of the BJP in UP during the 2019 election was largely shaped by the Hindutva ideology of the party. The party's strategy to form a big non-Yadav and non-Jatav social block in UP successfully challenged the SP–BSP Mahagathbandhan.[10] This Mahagathbandhan had attained success in the UP by-polls before the 2019 parliamentary election.[11] This was why political analysts were looking with big expectations towards this alliance. But the alliance did not work well. One of the reasons behind this, as discussed earlier, was that the BJP had already planned a strategy to counter it and started forming a broader non-Yadav and non-Jatav backward-caste social alliance.

As a step in this direction, on 6 August 2018 the Parliament passed a bill to grant constitutional status to the National Commission for Backward Classes as an answer to several members in the Rajya Sabha who urged the government to make public the findings of the caste census and implement reservation accordingly. This gave the commission powers to enforce the safeguards provided to the Socially and Educationally Backward Classes (SEBCs), particularly to address the grievance of the OBCs who until then had had to turn to the National Commission for the Scheduled Castes.[12]

In 2001, when Rajnath Singh of the BJP was chief minister of UP, a committee had been formed to review the reservation processes of SC and OBC communities. This committee was named the Social Justice Committee. It was headed by Hukum Singh, a cabinet minister in Singh's ministry.[13] In its 200-page report submitted in 2001, this committee suggested to divide SCs in two layers: Group A, that may contain Jatav and Dhusia castes, and Group B, including all other SC castes. This report recommended 10 per cent reservation for

Group A and 11 per cent for Group B. For the OBC category, it further suggested three categories: Group A would contain Yadavs and Ahirs and they would be given 5 per cent reservation, Group B would contain castes like Jats, Kurmis, Lodhs, Gujjars and this group may get 9 per cent reservation, and Group C would contain the most backward communities, for whom 14 per cent reservation was recommended (that is, a total of 28 per cent reservation for the OBC castes).[14]

All these efforts failed in UP because the Allahabad High Court prevented the implementation of these recommendations on the basis of a legal argument that quota within quota was not legally viable. But these efforts may be observed as one of the early attempts to officially delineate the multiple categories among the SCs and OBCs, who were hitherto seen as homogeneous communities, although they are quite heterogeneous.

It is true that a few castes among the SCs have acquired the capacity to aspire for a better life due to various historical reasons. SCs like

Jatavs and Pasis have acquired the capability to get education and claim government jobs before other numerically smaller Dalit castes.[15] Similarly, one may observe the case of Yadavs, Patels and Kurmis among the OBCs. These castes are numerically stronger, and thus in a beneficial position in democratic electoral processes. They assert their aspirations and try to achieve them. They have also produced community leaders, who have given voice to their desires and provided them visibility.

However, there are many castes among these communities that are still invisible. They are mostly uneducated and don't have their own community leaders to create pressure on the state. They are unable to assert their voice in democratic electoral politics, and thus have less representation in the state and politics. The benefits of state-led development projects reach them due to a trickle-down effect. They have not yet acquired sufficient capacity to take their due share in reservation-based policies. They are still knocking at the door of democracy.

In May 2018, some months before the announcement of 2019 parliamentary election, UP Chief Minister Yogi Adityanath constituted a committee called the Other Backward Classes Social Justice Committee[16] to give reservation to the most marginalized castes among the SCs and to the MBCs. The committee had, in its recommendations to the state government, favoured the division of OBC and Dalit sub-castes into three categories—pichhda (backward), ati-pichhda (very backward) and *sarvadhik pichhda* (most backward)—and provide quota within quota to them. Backward classes account for about 44 per cent of the electorate in the state and play a crucial role in making or marring political prospects of any party.[17] This created a debate in UP politics as this move of the CM was seen as a strategy to diminish the growing impact of the SP–BSP pact. It was also observed as a masterstroke of Yogi's to fracture the social alliance between OBCs and Dalits that was in the process of being created.

This political strategy of Yogi Adityanath to create a non-Yadav, non-Jatav OBC–SC mobilization worked well and it helped in accelerating the formation of social alliances during the 2019 election. To realize the benefits of this strategy, the Yogi Adityanath–led government in UP started working to implement this policy. This is the second phase of social justice politics in UP. It indicates that in the post-Mandal era, a new social justice politics is taking shape there. Similar policies have already been implemented in states like Tamil Nadu and Bihar, but the UP experiment with 'quota within quota' may inspire other Indian states to go on a similar path.

A few political analysts have raised doubts over the implementation of such policies and see legality as a hurdle. But it seems that the Yogi government had already done sufficient background research for its implementation. The government had held meetings with leaders of the most backward and most marginalized Dalit communities and alerted them of the move. An MBC leader of the BJP,

Anil Rajbhar, who was inducted into the Yogi cabinet, helped the government reach out to other MBC leaders and convince them to support the 'quota within quota' proposal. Reportedly, Yogi Adityanath told them to be vocal and defend the bill in the Assembly and on the streets. A team of bureaucrats and government legal counsels had already made plans if the matter were to go to the court at any stage.[18]

As of the time of writing, the planning department of UP, the social justice department and the State Planning Commission had provided available data to the bureaucrats who were working to prepare this bill. Thus, the Yogi Adityanath–led UP government has been making political, legal and administrative preparations. Politically speaking, 'quota within quota' will help the BJP bring non-Yadav OBCs and non-Jatav SCs into its fold faster. A larger section of the Kurmi caste, which is identified as a developed OBC group in this policy scheme, already supports the BJP on this issue.

This move was bound to anger the Yadavs, who form the SP's vote base, but the BJP knew they were anyway unlikely to vote for it. The non-Yadavs among the OBCs form a major voting block and this policy would have solidified their support for the BJP in the state. Similarly, the non-Jatav castes among the SCs could together weaken the Jatav vote bank and up the BJP's winnability factor in the 2019 elections.

This move gave the BJP an upper hand over the SP and the BSP in the state. It also helped them influence Om Prakash Rajbhar–led Suheldev Bharatiya Samaj Party. The party had, in the past, accused the BJP government of not implementing the Samajik Nyay Samiti (Social Justice Committee) Report, which had advised for 'quota within quota' system for communities like the Rajbhar.[19]

The 'quota within quota' policy is expected to lead to three things. First, it will create a political fracture among the OBC and SC communities and help the BJP erode the SP and BSP voter base. Second, at the social level, it will help the MBCs and most marginalized Dalits become more vocal and assertive, thanks to their newfound political capital. Third, a section of these invisible and silent social communities can hope to get a share of jobs, education and become visible beneficiaries of development schemes.

Diverting the Aggressive Ambition of Power

Politics centred on state power is like riding a lion. At any time, the lion can eat the person riding it. So, after getting such an impressive victory in the 2019 parliamentary election, Hindutva politics is facing a challenge to create checks and balances on the aggressive desire for power that is growing among their cadres. So diverting them from the politics of state power to the mission of shaping a society according to the RSS vision is now a big challenge for the Sangh, the BJP and their affiliates. The RSS talks about *samajik karya* (social work) even when what they do is a kind of social politics.

In the RSS agenda, 'social politics' means mobilizing communities and society in favour of the values and ideology of Hindutva politics through seva to people.

Prime Minister Narendra Modi, who has been trained in the Sangh culture, recently made a case for social politics or a politics that is sensitive to social activism.[20] In this, he drew on popular Hindu traditions, thinkers such as Vivekananda, leaders such as Deendayal Upadhyaya, and the RSS's own intellectual sources. The RSS defines politics mostly as social politics. While one can hold a critical view of the 'social' in Hindutva politics, in a broader sense, social politics has an expansive meaning.

At the time of the nationalist movement and even during the early years after Independence, electoral politics overlapped with social politics. Many great leaders of the movement, namely Mahatma Gandhi, Madan Mohan Malaviya, Maulana Abul Kalam Azad, Jawaharlal Nehru, Babasaheb Ambedkar, Sardar Patel, and so on, extended their battles to social movements to win political freedom and vice versa. In fact, the leaders of social reform movements were highly respected at the time of the nationalist movement and in the immediate post-Independence years. Simply put, the politics of state and nation-building was closely linked to social politics. The boundaries between social politics and electoral politics were flexible and often blurred.

Until the 1970s, leaders such as Ram Manohar Lohia, Indira Gandhi, Chaudhary Charan Singh, Chandrashekhar, Deendayal Upadhyaya and many leaders of regional parties were involved with various social movements. They recognized that the political mobilization that emerges from the womb of society leads to social rejuvenation, which is needed for good politics. These leaders had acquired a direct connect with the public through their involvement in social politics. Their charisma and public acceptance emerged from such engagement.

From the 1970s onwards, members of the mafia, criminals and petty businessmen began to enter politics. However, they were still not considered the main force in politics. Things began to change in the 1990s. After the launch of economic liberalization, market forces began to influence politics. All politics started turning into the politics of governance. The domain of politics began to be dominated by specialists like engineers, technocrats, financial managers and legal experts.

Further, this politics of governance became part of the politics of development. The politics of development was a complex affair that needed experts of various kinds. Politicians soon became dependent on these experts via bureaucrats to run the development machinery. Working with the bureaucrats as officers on special duty and advisers, the experts began to heavily influence the planning process. In many political parties, a group of managers, those with public relations know-how, financial expertise, IT knowledge as well as retired bureaucrats emerged as organizers of the parties. Many of them began to acquire key positions in government due to their proximity to the politicians; thus, advocates, technocrats, financial experts, economists, and so on, started getting ministry berths. However, these experts-turned-leaders were disconnected from the public, and in the name of the politics of governance/development, emerged as armchair politicians. Politics in the time of the neoliberal state became a politics of power, governance and development—losing, in the process, its social moorings. Many politicians stopped having a direct connect with the people. The task of working among people was outsourced to a new institution, namely the NGO, and politicians began to stay aloof from society. The social responsibilities of corporates were outlined, but no attempt was made to ascribe social responsibilities for politicians.

These politicians of 'Lutyens's Delhi'—a term Modi used extensively during his election campaigns—had no connect with the people. Big rallies, television debates and support in the media and social media at the time of elections were their only channels of communication with the public. The politics of democracy had turned into politics of state and power and, thereby, lost it social connect.

It was this lost tradition of politics as social work that Modi was alluding to when he spoke about the need to do social politics. And now when the RSS cadres express their desire for state power, the Sangh tries to turn their attention to this ideal. The social work the RSS does produces an impact that helps it influence people and politics. This is a form of 'social capital', as observed by a few political analysts.[21] It serves the RSS in its core agenda of extending the influence of Hindutva ideology within society, thus transforming politics from the grassroots.

Inventing New Areas of Social Politics

Political and social groups inspired by the Hindutva of the RSS are working on issues related with development ecology, environment and water.[22] Keeping the river in the backdrop as a source of water linked with both sacred and profane meanings, these groups are working to evolve a new social politics around various local, regional and great rivers of India such as the Ganga, Narmada, Brahmaputra and Godavari. For instance, recently Yogi Adityanath launched a huge social campaign around the Ganga in UP, named Ganga Yatra, to be held between 27 and 31 January. With sacredness at its essence, the Ganga is now being pushed to attain new meaning, towards refreshing environmental and developmental consciousness of the people. The communication around the Ganga Yatra was done through oral, aural, visual and ritual modes, in an attempt to interweave culture, economy and development. The Ganga Yatra would reassert traditional forms with modern content.

The Ganga Yatra was also an illustration of moving from the politics of state power to social politics, as suggested by Modi. He advised his party leaders, elected MPs and ministers to explore social issues as a way of engaging with people politically. In this, the

Ganga emerged as a potent combined symbol of culture, religion and socio-economic life. The river has a significant presence among the larger population of northern and central India, but it is symbolically present in most parts of India, where regional rivers also exist as tributaries to the Ganga and are worshipped as Ganga by the people there. The BJP's efforts to transform the social in the political and the political in the social in this manner illustrate a powerful craft of doing politics in a society like India.

The Ganga Yatra as a programme also provided an opportunity to the BJP to energize its cadres and reassemble their sympathizers and supporters. When any party remains in power for a long time, its cadres can become lazy and inactive. Taking its lesson from the weakening of the Congress due to its long presence in power, the BJP is alert and tries to develop such programmes so its cadres can reorganize and reunite. A party in power doesn't have the opportunity to do protest politics, which is usually how opposition parties conduct their mobilization; so, the party in power needs to evolve new issues to activate its leaders and followers.

The economic, social and cultural meanings of the Ganga appear to be inclusive, not divisive, unlike the Ram Janmabhoomi issue, so the BJP may have bigger plan to put the Ganga centre stage as an agenda of mobilizational politics. There are many sociocultural organizations that are working on various issues related to the Ganga. Various scattered socio-religious actions have also been initiated by saints and godmen and cultural–religious Hindu sects. Thus, the Ganga Yatra may enable a rainbow alliance of all such activities that are dispersed yet may form a cohesive forum for mobilization for the BJP as well as for a Hindutva-inspired state in UP and the country. It can also be seen as an effort to transform governmental efforts like Namami Gange—the national mission to clean the river—as social action. The BJP, drawing on the treasure of sociocultural resources in India, is quite competent and willing to evolve a mobilizational politics by transforming these through the vision of Hindutva.

In the BJP's new term from 2019 onwards, a major challenge for the RSS and Narendra Modi is to attain inclusivity through various programmes and policies, but their main problem is controlling the fringe saffron groups that are constantly disturbing the tone and tenor of the mainstream RSS and of the democratically elected BJP-led Central government. The power- and media-hungry politicians of the BJP itself and the fringe groups blunt the edge of social politics, which is Narendra Modi's tool of choice in his second term. He is acutely aware of this problem and warned the newly elected parliamentarians of his party about this in his address delivered just after the declaration of the result of the 2019 general election:

> A government is formed with people's mandate but keeping in mind the spirit of India's democracy, we have to remember that the government works with inclusion.

And that's why who said what during the campaigns is in the thing [sic] in the past for me now. We have to look forward and move forward along with everyone— even the opposition, for the benefit of the country. And that's why even after with this massive mandate we have to move forward with humility within the limits of the democracy.[23]

The Need for Social Leadership

Prime Minister Narendra Modi through his charismatic influence has evolved himself as a brand. He is proposing himself as a reference model and trying to lead Indian society in a certain direction.[24] It is interesting to observe that while doing politics of the state, he is also projecting himself as a social leader. So he is combining social politics and the politics of the state. As an illustration, he recently became a brand ambassador for the fitness campaign, as though in response to a social cause. In fact, it is in keeping with the RSS vision that a healthy society helps build a healthy and strong nation. His campaign for yoga was part of the same logic. The celebration of Yoga Day and his doing different yoga asanas on live television inspired a large number of his followers and impressed numerous others.

Through campaigns like Beti Bachao, Beti Parhao (save your daughter, educate your daughter), he tried to create a social campaign rather than a campaign of the administration and the state. In *Mann Ki Baat*, a radio programme in which the prime minister shares his thoughts with listeners, he gives the impression of focusing on social problems and of developing a discourse to inculcate human values in society, as per the Sangh's ideology. Along with being a politician and a statesman, Modi asserts himself also as a social leader, one who is constantly trying to strengthen his social moorings. His campaigns like the Swachh Bharat Abhiyan (Clean India Mission) and polythene-free nation are positioned as social campaigns.

As discussed earlier, from 1947 to the 1980s, most of the eminent political leaders were close to the public; they had an intimate relationship with their constituencies. These leaders emerged as mass leaders due to their oratorical skills and charismatic image that easily influenced the people. Indira Gandhi, Babu Jagjivan Ram, Chandrashekhar, Raj Narain, V.P. Singh and some others were leaders who had direct contact with the people, and thus were able to better understand their desires and aspirations.

When, from the 1990s, the concept of political leadership changed and various experts entered the fray, being popular among the public was no longer the sole criterion to become a political leader. This situation is still prevalent in the Indian political scenario. This gap demands a form of new politics, one where there is constant direct interaction between political leadership and the people. When people's local and micro socio-economic issues are heard, it provides the social linkages to democratic governance, which then provide the basis for larger policy changes.

Social leadership, which takes into account our day-to-day problems, is the need of the hour. In our recent survey in various parts of UP, we found that people did not want the leaders who are talking about them only on TV. They want the presence of these leaders in their daily life. A middle-aged person of Shahabpur village near Prayagraj told me that 'Indiraji remembered names of the people of my village. Whenever, someone from my village went to meet her, she used to ask about my father. Now, we no longer have leaders like her. Leaders of today are only visible on TV and Facebook'.[25] Another villager told me very specifically that *'Neta aisa ho jo sirf netagiri hi na kare, woh samaj ke liye kuchh kare'* (A leader should be one who is not just a political leader but also works for society). For the people who live in villages and small towns, flyovers and six-lane roads are not so important. A new brand of social politics has to raise issues like the unavailability of fertilizers, irrigation problems, loan issues, rising prices and other social issues that directly affect the larger society that is mostly comprised of farmers and lower-income groups working in the informal sector. A young student from a village near Prayagraj said, '*Bijli, pani, sadak* [electricity, water, roads] were important to us ten years ago. Now, issues related to smaller things[26] are more important for us.'

People today aspire for leaders who will interact with them directly, not from a distance. They are looking for leaders with whom they can share their life's ups and downs. This expectation is not limited to the villages. Even in cities and towns, people want a new kind of politics that can represent their desires and needs related to their livelihood. The proponents of Hindutva politics observe these desires among the people and are trying to respond to them in their own way. Prime Minister Narendra Modi is a political leader who keeps a grip on the pulse of the people. On one hand, he is trying to propose a mass politics that may associate with people's desires and, on the other, he wants to handle the ongoing crisis among his cadres and leaders who are inclined towards becoming power mongers and socially insensitive. He is also attempting to fill the lack being felt by the public by emerging as a social leader.

In addition to claiming a turn towards making politics more social than conventionally 'political', PM Modi has also been trying to include radical thinkers like Ambedkar and Lohia in his statecraft to build what he calls 'New India'. This has enabled him to create trust in his leadership among a wide base of people. However, as all this is done to forward the Hindutva ideology, it remains to be seen whether this brand of social politics will be inclusive.

CONCLUSION

Although the RSS declares that it is not a political organization, it can be clearly observed that their cadres and sympathizers help in organizing the elections for the BJP. From collecting feedback for the BJP candidates who contest elections or about candidate performance, helping the party to resolve contradictions and disillusionment among the cadres and leaders of the BJP, pursuing disenchanted social groups and communities to retain their goodwill for the BJP and escorting voters from their home to the booth, one may find RSS cadres helping the BJP in various ways during the elections. In fact, it appears that without the help and support of the RSS cadres, it would be very difficult for the BJP to manage elections. No other political party in India has the support of an organization like the RSS that the BJP has.

In politics, the groups that developed an appetite to include others, appropriate contradictions and synthesize the forces of its opposition, grew and expanded. One has to create a balance in the process of inclusion as well as appropriation. If the balance is disturbed in this process, the political groups face friction, fractures and ruptures in their political body and soul. We need to see how Hindutva politics, in the process of its constant expansion, deals with the making of a near-flawless balance between various contradictory elements and evolves a metanarrative that attempts to provide space to its various inner and outer contradictions and oppositions.

In the present times, democratic elections in India appear to be a war of narratives. Every political party invents its own ideological, political and historical resources to create its own narratives. They weave these narratives with the brand image of its star campaigner or main leader. In the recent few parliamentary elections, Hindutva polity has explored narratives of national security, development, mobilizing Dalits and OBC castes, spreading Hindutva culture, celebrations and festivities of Hindu icons, appropriating icons of the national movement such as Ambedkar, Sardar Patel, Netaji Subhash Chandra Bose, Lal Bahadur Shastri, Madan Mohan Malaviya, etc., and shaping discourses around triple talaq and other modern reformations to impress a section of non-Hindu religious communities, such as Muslims. To handle the issue of caste during the elections, the BJP provided space to the leaders of OBC communities and SC groups and gave respect to the identity markers and icons of these communities. It also promised to provide further opportunity of social justice to the MBCs and most marginalized SCs through the 'quota within quota' policy. The BJP's stand on the recent Supreme Court judgment regarding sub-classification of reservation in the states was intended to make space for the party among Dalits.[1] Sometime earlier, the BJP-led NDA government had passed a bill in the Parliament to protect the SC/ST Act from any judicial intervention.[2] The BJP and the Sangh Parivar's well-thought-out programme to include and appropriate OBC and Dalit communities in Hindutva politics is based on strategies, such as providing political representation and symbolic inclusion. The BJP government under Narendra Modi is also working to transform these marginalized communities into aspirational communities that may go beyond their caste identity. The distribution and dissemination of state-led policies, programmes and benefits is creating aspirations among underdeveloped and marginalized people to develop themselves and acquire democratic benefits with the help of the state.

In this book, I have tried to analyse the staggering rise of the BJP in India in the past few decades, which has astounded ideologues and policymakers all over the world. The party, which was disliked by a section of opinion makers because of its unabashed right-wing ideology known as Hindutva, has emerged as the most popular political option for a large section of Indians, irrespective of categories like rich/poor, urban/rural, Brahmin/Dalit and landowners/labourers. I have tried to tell the story of how democracy was being reshaped by Hindutva politics during the 2014 and 2019 parliamentary elections. Based on my extensive fieldwork in different parts of India over several years, I also discussed how the forms and processes of Hindutva politics deal with the politics of democracy in India. The RSS and Narendra Modi, through their mantra of social politics, are trying to build social capital. This social capital may form a new republic on one hand, and on the other hand help the BJP forge a long-term relationship with the people.

EPILOGUE

Hindutva Public and Bio–Public
A Pandemic Criss-cross

Sometimes history plays chase with us and generates surprising and shocking events. While the RSS was deeply engaged in evolving a 'Hindutva public' in caste-ridden Indian society, through the creation of Hindutva common sense, and trying to include various caste fragments within the whole, a shocking turn appeared not only in India but all over the world: the global pandemic caused by the novel coronavirus COVID-19. It intervened in human society and drastically changed some parts of its fabric. It ruptured conventionally defined locations of the 'human being' in society and in the democratic state.

I recall two most important turning points in contemporary Indian history: 1990 (or the decade of the 1990s) and 2020. The decade of the '90s, which hastened process of globalization after the launch of economic liberalization in India provided us mobility, motion and cyber power. The coronavirus pandemic in 2020, all of a sudden created a check on our mobility and drastically changed the social norms and culture of 'normal' time. Some of the social trends that had emerged in the 1990s continued until 2020. This may be called *longue durée* impact of the 1990s. So, in one way, we can perceive 2020 as the break and rupture of that impact.

The COVID-19 pandemic caused a worldwide emergency and the consequent lockdown created a severe social and economic crisis in India. It caused painful and tragic displacement of poor labourers. This 'Corona time' was labelled '*vipat kaal*' (time of calamity) by the poor migrants who lost their jobs due to lockdown and were compelled to take the torturous journey back home. It also changed the meaning of social norms like caste that are considered deeply rooted in Indian society as a source of inequality and exclusion.

So, we wanted to know what sociopolitical changes emerged in this virus-centred time and space in our society. How did it affect the Sangh project of creating a Hindutva public; how did the intervention of the virus in social processes create new trajectories that criss-crossed its formation? To study such issues, we chose to speak with migrant labourers, who appeared to be the most vulnerable social community and included various castes and social categories, to understand the new social experiences in Indian society. These labourers generally migrate from their place of origin for different reasons. A strong one is the 'pull' factor, such as the question of survival or employment opportunities. Numerous past studies have supported the argument that a large number of people migrate from rural to urban areas due to 'push' factors, such as lack of job availability in rural areas. As per the 2011 Census, there are 45.36 crore internal migrants in India. It is estimated that UP accounts for nearly 25 per cent interstate migration and Bihar accounts for 14 per cent.[1] The section of migrant labourers is constituted by various castes and communities such as SCs, STs, OBCs as well as upper castes.

We did small-scale research among migrant labourers to understand how caste functions in Indian society during the time of disaster and emergency like a pandemic. Do such situations break, dilute or weaken the rigidity of caste in our society? Do they change its nature? This research was centred on workers who had returned from various urban places. It attempted to document changes in the inner content of caste in their everyday life in five different experiential locations and time: (a) at the workplace and destination of the migrant labourer, (b) in their life during lockdown and after loss of job, (c) during their painful journey home, (d) in their life during quarantine and (e) their experience of caste when they resettled in their village basti after completing their quarantine period. Methodologically speaking, these three months provided five different kinds of life conditions and set of experiences to the migrants.

We interviewed 215 migrants comprising Dalit, OBC and upper castes who had returned from places like Mumbai, Delhi, Surat and Pune to UP and Bihar. We selected six quarantine centres each in UP and Bihar to document the everyday life experience of migrants there.

Most respondents had completed their quarantine period either at a quarantine centre or at home and then reached their villages and towns. Our research associates interviewed them, mostly over the phone, and a few of them face to face, to know how caste identities remained with them at the destination and during the pandemic.

The research staff and our students helped us with the interviews. We developed a network of local informants from local journalists, local leaders and social activists to map and procure primary information, contact numbers and location details upon which our researchers developed interview strategies. For us, this is a 'methodology of emergency' as during the lockdown we could not go to the field for long-drawn-out participatory interviews. We were not able to engage with our respondents for longer discussions over the telephone either, which is needed in such research. As we were not able to read their faces and there were many things that they were unable to express in a cohesive manner, their responses were fragmented and fractured. But we had to weave them together. Sometimes they became silent, sometimes they cried, sometimes they just whispered. As researchers, first of all, we had to open their memory box and then search for all the mementos from the calamitous moments. This posed a major challenge for us as we were compelled to do most of the interviews telephonically. We are aware of the shortcomings of telephonic interviews but this pandemic had offered us a unique opportunity to understand the functioning of social norms, such as caste, in the time of a health emergency.

Most of the interviews and narratives that we collected from our respondents form various narrative types after content analysis.

These narrative types recur in several interviews. These are as follows: 'Type A' reveals flexibilities of caste claims of the migrants at their workplaces, 'Type B' reflects how caste became diluted during their return journey and in COVID-19 centres, and 'Type C' represents ruptures in vertical untouchability between the castes, the generation of a new experience of horizontal distance and a new kind of untouchability between bodies based on the fear of the virus. Here, I am deriving and submitting my observations using these narratives, which serve as illustrations of the different social processes unfolding during the virus-centred emergency.

Caste and the Pandemic

I am not going to delve into the debate on whether caste, which is framed in the Indian caste system, works according to ancient scripture or as per social tradition passed on from generation to generation, while accounting for certain changes based on time and context.[2] There is a popular belief among a section of people in India that caste will never completely disappear. And that it always works in the same way and form. We see caste, religion and other deeply entrenched, almost primordial, identities as the only source of forming group identities that determine the rules of exclusion in Indian society.[3]

Caste does not behave like a mathematical formula in Indian society. It is not fixed nor homogeneous, but very complex and complicated. It does not work merely as a defined structure but also as a *bhav*, which may be called '*jatibhav*'. 'Bhav' loosely translates as a combination of feeling-sentiment-affect; 'jatibhav', thus, is a *sensibility* of caste that has been observed in Indian society. These are feelings and sensibilities in the background, which may be evoked or mobilized in a certain direction. That is why, even as we analyse it through our intellectual-seeming commonsensical discourses, we find that it is not always rigid. It does not always work in the same way; our 'experiential capital' may make it appear diluted, flexible and even benign. It works in various degrees, following multiple ups and downs with changing time and context.

It is interesting to note that we don't consider the phenomenon of a time of emergency when we conceptualize our social processes. However, our traditional discourse considers the rupturing and subversion of 'normal' social norms during times of emergency, which is called *aapad dharma*. In the *Chandogya Upanishad*, there is a story of Chakrayana Usasti:

The famine had spread in Chakrayana Usasti's village. He had been starving for two consecutive days. Thus, he decided to travel to another village but the situation was the same in that village. He moved from there and found a man sitting under a tree. The man was eating something by licking it. Usasti went to that person and asked, 'What are you eating?' The man answered, 'I am eating *udad* [dal].' Usasti asked the man to give him some as he had been starving for two days. The man said, 'I would have surely given you, but it is defiled now.' Usasti said, 'Let it be defiled, please give me some of it.' The man gave some udad to Usasti. The man also had a pot of water with him. He drank some from it touching his mouth to it, and left some for Usasti. But after finishing the udad, Usasti stood up and started to walk away. The man said, 'Leave after drinking some water.' To which Usasti replied, 'I don't drink defiled water.' The man asked, 'You can eat defiled udad so why can't you drink defiled water?' Usasti answered, 'If I would have not eaten that defiled udad, I would have died. Now, I have some energy. I will drink water from any nearest waterfall.'[4]

As per the story, Usasti ate the udad following aapad dharma. It is true that aapad dharma fails to continue in the normal time, but it does generate social experiences that last in social memory and affect society for a long time.

Both the characters in this story are not merely actors in a theatrical play who played their role without being influenced by the actions. In real life, any social action will change both: the one who initiates the act and the other who responds to it. The social action even as per aapad dharma, as described in this stereotypical story, may have its long-term influence. The experience does not always go futile; it changes us to some degree. The pandemic forced many to follow the norms of aapad dharma, and the experiences that evolved during this time may remain within us even during normal times. How the experiential capital operates within the inner worlds of individuals may affect social processes slowly and silently for a long time.

In fact, emergency time can write a completely new sociology and compel us to redefine society and human existence in new ways. This coronavirus-centred time may be temporary but it has transformed us from social body to bare biological body, which is explained by eminent thinker Giorgio Agamben as 'worry for bare life in the center of our concern'. 'Bare life' is a life where the main concern of the human being is the biological body and it precedes any other social concern. In this time of the coronavirus pandemic, bare life and the danger of losing it formed new social combinations and fractured and diluted social equations based on primordial identities even in Indian society.[5]

In this research we tried to observe whether and how the social norms of normal times may change during an emergency such as this one. These changes may ultimately not sustain for long but the experiential capital has been gathered. Exploring the memories of the migrant labourers, which revealed how they remembered their experiences, was critical to this research. In the everyday process of social life, whatever remains in people's memories functions as experiential capital.

We observed that the conventional perception that caste identities become weaker in the workplaces of migrants, especially in cosmopolitan cities, may be partly true. Our research suggests that these migrants present their caste identity in their places of work in clever forms. They use, reuse, hide and play with their own caste identities as per their requirements. They sometimes use it to garner social and political support in the localities where they live. Sometimes they hide it if they find that their caste may create trouble for them. We also find many cases where some of the migrants claim a 'higher' identity as their strategy for survival. For instance, a migrant Shila belongs to the Dalit caste and works in Surat as a household help. She narrated how she strategically deals with her caste identity when she goes to ask for work. She said, *'Jahaan jaisa jarurat lage wahaan waise batayi.'* (I spoke of my identity according to what was required in a particular house.) 'In our basti in Surat where most of us were from the lower caste, we didn't hide or wrongly inform about our caste, but to the "saheb house", we used to hide it and claim to be from castes such as Yadav, Kahar.'[6] Her husband, Devidin, narrated another interesting use of caste identity at the workplace. He said, 'There was a leader in Surat who belongs to UP.

He was from the OBC community and was very influential there. He used to give all his support to me. He was under the impression that I too am an OBC from UP.'[7]

So, caste for migrants, especially poor workers, appears to be an instrument that they use strategically; most of the time, it remains with them in a benign form. They keep accommodating and adjusting their identity based on the context, because their main struggle at the place of work is of survival. So, in the city of work, caste identities of the migrants do not appear as rigid and assertive in most of the cases, but operate as flexible, strategic and instrumental.

This pandemic and the subsequent lockdown, which took away their jobs, led to a painful journey of return, followed by quarantine in their hometown or village. They had to nearly forget their caste. Most of their experiences reveal that '*Jaan bachawe aur ghar pahuchne ki chinta ke saamne aur kuchh nahi sujhat rahe*' (Apart from worrying about our lives and reaching home, we could think of nothing else). Second, untouchability at the vertical level between different castes became almost invisible. An OBC youth said that in those difficult times they all became one caste: *'dukhiyaron ka caste'* (the caste of the miserable).[8] We learnt about many incidents where people from the upper castes took food and water from the hands of fellow Dalits and OBC migrant travellers during their long journey. One vulnerable poor upper-caste youth told us: *'Uss wakt jaat nahi yaad aata tha'* (Caste did not come to mind at that time). He said that only their village and family were on their minds in those days, and they wanted simply to save their lives and reach home.[9] One Dalit respondent asked in response to one of our questions, *'Vipat ke maare ki kya jaat, bhaiyya?'* (What is the meaning of caste for a sufferer of such disaster?) In response to our question that whether despite the fear they sat together while waiting for transport or in front of a registration office, he said, 'Sometimes, even when we sat or stood at a distance, we would borrow *khaini* [chewing tobacco] from others.'[10]

Another form of social experience emerged in the interviews about their journeys home from the place of work. Ram Pratap Chourasia from Kaushambi district in UP has been working in Mumbai for many years with his son and younger brother. He said that when lockdown started, 'we became jobless and started starving. There was no transportation available for us to return home so we decided to return by foot. Sometimes we got a lift in a truck for some distance. We got a cart on the way which also helped us cover some distance. So, by foot, truck, cart and other means we reached Kaushambi in five days. The truck driver was Muslim. He gave us food and water too. On the way we met many drivers of trucks and carts who were Muslim. They allowed us to sit in their vehicle and offered us water and food.'[11] From their narratives it appears there was no untouchability and vertical distance based on caste during that difficult time. Water, food and goods were moving hand to hand without anyone asking about caste. That they helped and provided emotional support to each other without considering each other's caste emerged as one of the main trends of migrants' behaviour. When they entered a quarantine centre, caste consciousness, which had become diluted and benign during travel, may have reappeared among some of them, but we have documented various instances where members of various castes ate and stayed together, forgetting untouchability.

Most of the respondents revealed that when they entered their bastis after completing the quarantine, the relationship between the migrants of various castes appeared to be different from normal times. The memory of suffering plays an important role in reshaping the meaning of their identity. Now, they seem to have a mixed identity in villages—the combination of caste and the experience of a worker who has suffered the jolts produced by the coronavirus. Now caste works within them in a diluted and benign form.

Another new form of caste combination emerged in some of the villages, which may be seen as a rupture in routine behaviour. In one village near Samastipur, Bihar, when a Dalit opposed a migrant from the upper caste who had entered the village escaping quarantine, members of the upper castes supported the Dalit due to their own fear of the coronavirus. Here, safety from infection became more important than (traditional) caste solidarity. One can observe a slow transformation of identities from 'caste public' to 'bio-public'. In this, the concerns of caste are being overpowered by the concerns of the biological body and its safety.

Yet another form of social distancing and untouchability emerged during quarantine. Dhananjay Dixit, age thirty years, from a village in Bundelkhand district works in Mumbai. He returned from Mumbai to his village in the lockdown period. He observed fourteen days' quarantine under a tree in the field of his village. For his society, he was more than untouchable for at least those fourteen days and was viewed with hostility. People called him 'Corona'. His wife was prevented by people of his own caste from taking water from the village handpump. They did not allow her to even touch its handle.

Many such experiences may remain in the consciousness of the suffering migrants, from different castes, and may weaken caste identities for at least some time.[12]

In a village called Lakhipur, there is a family of Brahmins with the surname Shukla. They live with Dalit and MBC communities, some of whom identify as Harijan, Arakh, Khengar, etc. A few from the Yadav caste also stay in this village. A youth of the Shukla family works in Mumbai. He returned during lockdown, completed his quarantine and returned to the basti. Now, no one from among the Dalit, MBC or OBC people of this village allow any member of this family to either touch or come close to anyone. The family can't even sit in a public space, such as a temple or the village pond. It is interesting to note that before the pandemic, the same Brahmin family did not allow these Dalit and MBCs to touch them or come close. In other words, during normal times, the Dalits were untouchable for the Shukla family, while now the Shukla family has turned untouchable for the Dalits, MBCs and others.

So, the virus has upturned the pyramid of the Indian caste system in this way.[13]

Cases of untouchability within the family also emerged. The mother–son relationship is considered highly emotional and deep in Indian society. In family stories and in folk songs, the mother is always considered devoted towards the son and sometimes sons are portrayed as the betrayer of their mother's trust. One can see something different in this case from a village in Bundelkhand. Ram Khelawan Yadav, who worked in Surat, returned to the village during lockdown. He had to do twenty-one days' home quarantine in his own house. Ram Khelawan's uncle and brothers decided that he would stay in the room in the courtyard in which his mother was living. When the mother came to know about this, she showed her annoyance and opposed this arrangement saying that old people were more vulnerable to COVID-19 infection. Her anxiety for the safety of her biological body had affected her socially conditioned sense of motherly sacrifice.[14]

We can see how the emergency time pushed back some of our routine behaviours and modes of relating with others. Keeping the bare biological body safe from infection and preventing any contact became the centre of concern for everyone. At least for some time, the coronavirus displaced caste from our social discourse and pushed it to the secondary level. A different kind of untouchability appeared at the horizontal level, functioning body to body, and made vertical untouchability between castes, secondary. This does not mean that in the quarantine centres or in villages caste untouchability did not make its appearance at all. But that caste identities can also mutate in a changing context and express themselves at different temperatures, not always remaining the same.

It is true that caste is deeply ingrained in our social system. But an emergency like a pandemic gives jerks and shocks to this system. It sometimes ruptures its normal and routine nature. It breaks multiple dichotomies between various caste-based categories and sometimes forms surprising combinations. The emotional capital from suffering in the emergency remains part of our identities for a long time; it may work slowly to reduce caste-based arrogance and reshape our caste identities in subtle and invisible ways. While in India, we may read any social event from conflicting caste angles, experiential capital that can in fact evolve social unity also remains part of the social process, which needs to be considered.

Due to the fear of infection, social distancing might become a long-term strategy for human survival and it may gradually transform into a social mode of Indian life. This may enthuse a kind of social habit among us to perceive 'otherness' less at the level of caste and more at the level of the biological body. The fear of getting sick, having to lead a lonely life and the danger of losing it will be at the core of our existential reality and identity for at least a few years. It may eradicate some of our entrenched, ancient social habits and invent new social attitudes. So, various forces in Indian society that derive ideological resources from the caste system may mutate and acquire a new form.

Hindutva Public, Bio-Public and the RSS

The process of the making of Hindutva public got ruptured by the outbreak of the coronavirus pandemic. It turned the entire attention of society from identity to survival. Even the initiator of the Hindutva public, such as the RSS and its allied organizations, reframed their efforts, agendas and activities, guided by the requirements of this emergency time. It is indeed a new situation for any sociocultural–political agency and its long-term project. But these agencies tended to reformulate their strategies and came up with responses to the new situation.

The RSS responded by carrying out seva for the vulnerable and the sufferers of the pandemic. Seva remained one of the main sources of dissemination of Sangh ideology to the people and for continuing to strengthen the organization.

Seva karya is very important in the making of the RSS. One of the pracharaks told me that wherever they have expanded, it is only because of their seva karya. The Sangh, through its seva agenda, negotiated with this new formation of a bio-public. It appeared with new seva schemes to provide protective gear, such as masks, sanitizers, soap, herbal potions, and other immunity-building Ayurvedic supplements and medicines. Ayurvedic supplements were distributed in middle- and upper-class-dominated housing societies and bastis by the local units of the Sangh in states like Maharashtra, Madhya Pradesh, Delhi and Gujarat. Food packets and water were planned to be distributed in the slums and among the displaced migrant labourers. The agenda for initiating various social actions aimed at protecting the body from the virus became a central concern of the Sangh and its affiliated organizations. Any polarizational act was opposed by the BJP leaders and the Sangh's important pracharaks themselves declared that their main concern at the moment was to protect people from the virus. Many eminent leaders of the BJP, such as J.P. Nadha and Rajnath Singh, as well as Sangh leaders opposed any effort at communalization of the virus.[15] In this way, the Sangh gave new form to its already honed seva karya agenda to link itself with the formation of this new fear-induced bio-public in India.

When the pandemic will be controlled and social life returns to normal, the RSS may forge an easy link between these two formations—the Hindutva public and the bio-public—within one individual. The RSS may work not to allow any conflict between these two formations; its presence in both may help it to transform the newly emerged bio-public of the pandemic time into the Hindutva public of normal time. The Sangh's initiatives to project Indian values and propagate yoga and Ayurveda as the main immunity-building constituents for Indians may be seen as an attempt to negotiate with the new reality. If this biological concern prevails for a longer time as a dominant concern, it may hamper the making of the Hindutva public. However, in a post-corona time, the RSS and its affiliates would like to submerge the biological anxieties of the people by projecting Hindutva values and lifestyle as powerful protectors of human bodies against the virus.

ACKNOWLEDGEMENTS

This book has evolved from my opinion pieces published from time to time in newspapers and digital sites such as *The Hindu*, *Indian Express*, *Outlook*, *Economic and Political Weekly*, *DailyO.in*, *News18.com*, *CatchNews.com*, and other forums. These articles served as a plot to develop the bigger story of Hindutva politics, which I was documenting between 2014 and 2019 in northern India. I express my sincere thanks to the editors of these newspapers and websites for publishing my pieces.

I am grateful to Penguin Random House India and its commissioning editor Richa Burman for showing interest in this work, and for her work on the manuscript. I express my sincere thanks to Mousumi Majumder who helped me in editing the first draft. I am very grateful to Archana who helped me in the creation of these pieces, with the fieldwork related to these studies and during the entire journey of this book. I thank Swadesh Singh and Ramanand for their comments on various issues related to the Sangh. I also thank my office staff for their constant support. Needless to say, any faults in the book are entirely mine.

NOTES

Introduction

1. 'Adivasi vs Vanvasi: The Hinduization of Tribals in India', *Outlook*, 20 November 2002, excerpted from the report, *Foreign Exchange of Hate: IDRF and the American Funding of Hindutva* (Mumbai, India: Sabrang Communications & Publishing Pvt. Ltd, and France: The South Asia Citizens Web, 2002).
2. 'Mohan Bhagwat in Overdrive to Portray RSS as Inclusive, Evolving Organisation', *TheWire. in*, 19 September 2018.
3. 'In sociological terms, this is yet another blow to those who peddle illusions about the power of caste and regional politics. Those identities are breaking down': in Pratap Bhanu Mehta, 'Staggering dominance: The only authentic analysis of this election is two words—Narendra Modi', *Indian Express*, 24 May 2019.

Chapter 1: Reinventing the RSS: Perception and Reality

1. 'Ram Ki Shakti Puja', in *Anamika*, first published in *Bharat*, 1937 (Delhi: Rajkamal Prakashan, 2004). English translation by Madhu B. Joshi.
2. *Business Today*, 18 June 2019.
3. Pragya Kaushika, 'The RSS supports homosexual and transgender rights, frowns on live-in relationships', ANI, 20 September 2019, https://www.aninews.in/news/national/general-news/rss-supports-homosexual-and-transgender-rights-frowns-on-live-in-relationships20190920215149/.
4. He reiterated this at his historic speech in Nagpur on 15 October 1956, a day after he had embraced Buddhism. For the original statement made in 1935 in Yeola, see Dhananjay Keer, *Dr. Ambedkar: Life and Mission* (Bombay: Popular Prakashan, 1971 [1954]), p. 253.
5. Including UP, Bihar, MP, Rajasthan, Chhattisgarh and Jharkhand.
6. *Business Standard*, 10 October 2015; *Asian Age*, 15 November 2015; and Kumar Shakti Shekhar, 'Ambedkar Jayanti: How PM Modi

won confidence of Dalits and Uttar Pradesh',
India Today, 14 April 2017.

7. Satyasundar Barik, '51% rise in shakhas since
    2010, says RSS', *The Hindu*, 16 October 2019.

8. Ramdhari Singh Dinkar, *Rashmirathi*
    (Allahabad: Lok Bharti Prakashan, 1952).

9. Pandit Giridhar Sharma Chaturvedi, '*Madan
    Mohan Malaviyaji ki Dharm Bhakti*', in
    Sammelan Patrika, Shraddhanjali visheshank,
    Hindi Sahitya Sammellan (Prayag, 1884),
    p. 12.

10. Field notes from 23 June 2017.

11. The MBC communities in this area are Darzis,
    Bhunjawas, Halwayis, Tamers, Chauhans,
    Pals, Nishads, Rajaks, Sens, Patwaris, Balmikis,
    Banskars, Baras, Raickwars, Dhimars, etc.

12. The nomadic communities include Nats,
    Kapariyas, Banjaras, Khairwars and Kabutaras;
    tribal communities include Sahariyas, Gonds
    and Kols; and other most marginalized SC
    communities include Khatiks, Mehtars,
    Noniyas, etc.

13. Ibid.

14. 'Religion is the sigh of the oppressed creature,
    the heart of a heartless world, and the soul
    of soulless conditions. It is the opium of

the people.' Karl Marx, *Critique of Hegel's 'Philosophy of Right'*, ed. Joseph O'Malley, trans. Annette Jolin and Joseph O'Malley (New York: Cambridge University Press, 1970); originally written by Marx in 1844. Available at: https://www.marxists.org/archive/marx/works/1843/critique-hpr/index.htm.

15. Badri Narayan, 'For Dalits and Tribals, Respect Means Equality in Religious Space as Well', *News18.com*, 12 November 2017, https://www.news18.com/news/india/opinion-for-dalits-and-tribals-respect-means-equality-in-religious-space-as-well-1574271.html. See chapter 2 for more on these sects.

16. Badri Narayan, *Women Heroes and Dalit Assertion in North India*, in *Cultural Subordination and the Dalit Challenge*, Vol. 5 (New Delhi: Sage Publications, 2006).

17. *Times of India*, 23 October 2015.

18. Badri Narayan, 'In Narendra Modi's model village, development has a caste', *CatchNews.com*, 13 February 2017. The 'paravartan' campaign was given the moniker of *ghar wapsi* (homecoming) by the news media. Even though the temple had been built, development was yet to reach the Musahars

and other marginalized communities in the 'model' village when we had visited.

19. 'UP CM Yogi Adityanath says good news may come soon while inaugurating Ram Katha in Gorakhpur', *Hindustan Times*, 5 October 2019.

20. 'To counter BJP might, Mamata Banerjee announces formation of "Jai Hind Vahini" and "Banga Janani Samiti"', *Financial Express*, 31 May 2019.

21. 'Rahul Gandhi: We are defeating BJP in ideological fight', *National Herald*, 13 February 2019.

Chapter 2: Appropriation As Process: Caste, Dalits and Hindutva

1. From 'Ram Ki Shakti Puja', *Anamika*, 1937. Translated into English by Madhu V. Joshi.

2. *Amar Ujala* (UP), 26 December 2019.

3. Malini Bhattacharjee, *Disaster Relief and the RSS: Resurrecting 'Religion' through Humanitarianism* (New Delhi: Sage, 2019), p. 268.

4. Ibid.

5. From a discussion with RSS cadres in Prayagraj and Varanasi between 2017 and 2019.

6. *Amar Ujala*, 5 October 2016, p. 17.

7. Badri Narayan, *Fascinating Hindutva: Saffron Politics and Dalit Mobilisation* (New Delhi: Sage Publications, 2009), pp. 80–81.

8. Ibid., pp. 80–85.

9. Ibid., pp. 137–57.

10. *Amar Ujala*, 12 April 2016.

11. This happened most noticeably after the failure of the Janata Party–led government (post-Emergency), when the plank of the non-Congress socialists started to fail. The political alternatives for the OBCs started to blur, and some of them began to shift towards non-Congress Hindutva politics.

12. See chapter 1 for details.

13. There was a lot of hue and cry after the Supreme Court's verdict on reservations in promotions on 7 February 2020, in *Mukesh Kumar & Anr. vs The State of Uttarakhand & Ors.* On 16 February, the Bhim Army took out a protest march against this ruling. PTI, *India Today*, https://www.indiatoday.in/india/story/bhim-army-chandrashekhar-azad-protest-sc-reservation-promotions-1647109-2020-02-16.

14. H. Dwivedi, *Kabir: Kabir ke Vyaktitva, Sahitya aur Darshanik Vichaaron ki Alochana* (New Delhi: Rajkamal Prakashan, 2014).

15. Binay Kumar Pattnaik, 'Tribal Resistance Movements and the Politics of Development-Induced Displacement in Contemporary Orissa in Social Change', *Social Change*, 43:1, 5 April 2013, pp. 53–78.

16. Smita Gupta, 'How the RSS grew roots in the North-East', *The Hindu Businessline*, 9 March 2018.

17. 'Adivasi vs Vanvasi: The Hinduization of Tribals in India', *Outlook*, 20 November 2002, excerpted from the report, *Foreign Exchange of Hate: IDRF and the American Funding of Hindutva* (Mumbai, India: Sabrang Communications & Publishing Pvt. Ltd, and France: The South Asia Citizens Web, 2002).

18. 'Tribals' "ghar wapsi" a bid to save identity: RSS wing', *Times of India*, 22 December 2014.

19. Mayank Aggarwal, 'Despite controversies on tribal issues, BJP wins in tribal constituencies', *Mongabay.com*, 31 May 2019.

20. Interview with Manojji, Sangh pracharak, Kashi Pranta, UP, 2017.

21. Ibid.

22. Ibid.

23. Vasant Moon, *Dr Babasaheb Ambedkar, Writings and Speeches*, Vol. 5 (Bombay: Government of Maharashtra, 1979).
24. Field Diary.
25. This is based on our discussions with a few activists of these organizations working in UP.
26. Field Diary, 2018.
27. See section on religious space and influence in chapter 1 for more details.
28. Interview with Satyendraji, 2018.
29. Jhuriya, Sahabpur, UP, 2005.
30. Interview with Satyendraji, 2018.

Chapter 3: Forging a New Mobilizational Consciousness

1. Interview with Manojji, 3 May 2018.
2. K.N. Panikkar, 'The Hindutva Ride', *Frontline*, 2010. https://frontline.thehindu.com/editors-pick/the-hindutva-ride/article33036001.ece
3. *Hindustan Times*, 20 February 2017.
4. V.N. Rai, *Combating Communal Conflicts* (Allahabad: Anamika Prakashan, 1998).
5. Suman Layak and Indulekha Aravind, 'How fringe organisations like Hindu Sena and Sanatan Sanstha are attempting to set the

agenda with BJP in power', *Economics Times*, 8 November 2015.

6. Rai, *Combating Communal Conflicts*, p. 61.

7. The Muzaffarnagar riots of August–September 2013 are an example of this. Utkarsh Anand, 'SC holds Akhilesh govt guilty of negligence, orders arrest of all Muzaffarnagar accused', *Indian Express*, 26 March 2014, https://indianexpress.com/article/india/india-others/sc-holds-akhilesh-govt-guilty-of-negligence-orders-arrest-of-all-muzaffarnagar-accused/.

8. 'Express Investigation Part-I: Over 600 "communal incidents" in UP since LS results, 60% near bypoll seats', *Indian Express*, 5 August 2014.

9. T. Brass (ed.), *New Farmer's Movements in India* (Ilford: Frank Cass, 1995).

10. N. Bajpai, 'Muslims to decide political fortunes in Uttar Pradesh?' *New Indian Express*, 2 February 2019.

11. 'Express Investigation Part-II', 6 August 2014.

12. 'Express Investigation Part-IV', 8 August 2014.

13. Some villages of UP where these small clashes took place were village Gaineridan, Mohalla Malkand (Hardoi), Kalasi Lane (Saharanpur), Badarpur, Kheti Viran, Kheti Sarai, Kant

(Moradabad), Lisadi (Meerut), Ashapur (Faizabad), Neta Nagar (Kaushambi), Kasba (Shamli) and Mohalla Naurangabad East (Hathras). Source: 'Express Investigation Part-III', 7 August 2014.

14. 'RSS claims two lakh new recruits in western U.P.', *The Hindu*, 24 February 2018.

15. Walter K. Andersen and Shridhar D. Damle, *The Brotherhood in Saffron: The Rashtriya Swayamsevak Sangh and Hindu Revivalism* (Gurgaon: Penguin Random House India, 2019 [originally published by Westview Press, 1987]).

16. 'Express Investigation Part-III', 7 August 2014.

17. Ibid.

18. Sudha Pai, 'Future of Dalit Politics Swings between Decline and Regeneration', *TheWire. in*, 25 March 2020.

19. Piyush Rai and Priyangi Agarwal, 'If they have faith in Ali, we have Bajrang Bali, says Yogi', *Times of India*, 10 April 2019.

20. Badri Narayan, 'Hindutva back on BJP's agenda', *Mint*, 13 August 2013.

21. Ibid.

22. Ibid.

23. Ibid.

24. Ibid.
25. Ibid.
26. Ibid.
27. Vivek Suredran, 'Politics of lynching, the new normal in India', *India Today*, 27 July 2017.

Chapter 4: The RSS in Elections: Political and Apolitical

1. In 'Java Meier', in *The Collected Short Stories of Bertolt Brecht*, eds John Willett and Ralph Manheim (New York: Bloomsbury, 2015).

2. Among these were Citizens for Accountable Governance (CAG) led by Prashant Kishor (as reported in Sruthijith K.K., 'Meet the nonprofit whose backroom worked powered Modi to victory', *Scroll.in*, 18 June 2014), and Oglivy and Mather (as reported in *Economic Times* in Pritha Mitra Dasgupta, 'BJP advertising campaign to go live this weekend', 7 March 2014 and 'From Narendra Modi to Brand Modi: Meet the team behind BJP's unprecedented poll campaign', 1 May 2014). See chapter 4 for more on the CAG.

3. Nairita Das, 'RSS Shocker: Mohan Bhagwat refuses to cross limit for Narendra Modi',

OneIndia.com, 11 March 2014, https://www.oneindia.com/india/election-shocker-rss-cant-cross-limit-for-narendra-modi-mohan-bhagwat-1410167-lse.html.

4. Badri Narayan, 'Modi's Modus Operandi in the 2014 Elections', *Economic and Political Weekly*, Vol. 49, No. 20, 17 May 2014, pp. 12–14. A large part of this chapter has been adapted from this article. Where citation is not provided, this article is the source of the information.

5. Narayan, 'Modi's Modus Operandi'; Archis Mohan, 'RSS steps in to work for Modi's victory and its own survival', *Business Standard*, 25 April 2014; and R. Jagannathan, 'How the RSS is heavily invested in elections 2014 and Modi', *Firstpost.com*, 24 March 2014.

6. 'The Namo Rath: Playing near them, 54-inch Narendra Modi', *Indian Express*, 23 March 2014.

7. Badri Narayan, 'RSS moves out of the back office', *Mint*, 30 August 2013.

8. Ibid.

9. See chapter 3 for details.

10. Rahi Gaikwad, 'Serial blasts rock Modi's rally venue in Patna, five killed', *The Hindu*, 27 October 2013.

11. Narayan, 'Modi's Modus Operandi', and field notes.

12. Darshan Desai, 'The minds behind Modi's "achhe din" and "Chai pe Charcha" campaign', *India Today*, 21 May 2014, https://www.indiatoday.in/elections/gujarat/story/the-minds-behind-modis-achhe-din-and-chai-pe-charcha-campaign-193764-2014-05-21.

13. The local RSS cadres involved in the election campaign also had all the details.

Chapter 5: Politics, Narratives and Elections

1. Omar Rashid, 'Modi hits back on "fake OBC" jibes, says he is "most backward"', *The Hindu*, 27 April 2019.

2. Badri Narayan, 'Caste narratives have emerged as an important trope in the 2019 election', *Indian Express*, 30 April 2019.

3. 'Adityanath compares polls to a contest between Ali and Bajrang Bali', *Scroll.in*, 10 April 2019.

4. 'Both Ali, Bajrang Bali ours, says Mayawati; links her community to Hanuman', PTI and *Economic Times*, 13 April 2019.

5. Even though Nitish benefited from the vote of the upper castes, he did not allow this alliance

to dilute his development agenda or caste agenda. This proved to be his strength.

6. 'Kumbh Mela: Prayagraj becomes political melting pot as BJP goes on Hindutva overdrive to brace from Ayodhya uncertainty', *FirstPost. com*, 15 January 2019.

7. Interview with the RSS *zila karyvah*, Gangapar, Prayagraj, 28 October 2018.

8. 'Bill to restore original SC/ST atrocity law passed by Lok Sabha', *Economic Times*, 6 August 2018.

9. *Amar Ujala* (Lucknow), 25 December 2018.

10. Badri Narayan, 'Of Melas and Politics', *Indian Express*, 18 December 2018.

11. Ibid.

12. *The Hindu*, 12 June 2016.

13. A possible reason for this were that the Muslims were not fully satisfied with the efforts of SP to protect them during riots, although the SP spoke for them on various fronts. Another reason was that the BSP worked hard towards a Dalit–Muslim alliance and gave a large number of tickets to Muslims (see PTI, '113 upper caste, 97 Muslim candidates in BSP list', *The Hindu*, 8 January 2017). This created fragmentation among the SP's base Muslim votes.

14. Some of the important communities in this category include Saithwar, Bind, Gadariya, Nishad, Prajapati, Teli, Sahu, Koeri, Mali, Saini and Bharbhuja. See also chapter 1.

15. The Banjara, Tura, Kumhar, Kahar, Bhar, Prajapati, Rajbhar, Batham, Gaur, Manjhi, Mallah, Dheemar, Madhua, Kashyap, Kewat, Nishad and Bind.

16. 'SP, BSP Disrupt RS Proceedings Over UP OBC List', *Outlook*, 11 December 2013.

Chapter 6: The Road Ahead: Framing Own Public

1. 'The Solution', in *Poems, 1913–1965*, eds John Willet and Ralph Manheim (New York and London: Methuen, 1979), p 440.

2. 'History made, triple talaq bill passed by Parliament', *India Today*, 30 July 2019.

3. Kaushik Deka, 'How Kashmir changed on August 5', *India Today*, 6 August 2019.

4. Krishnadas Rajagopal, 'Ayodhya verdict: Temple at disputed site, alternative land for mosque, rules Supreme Court', *The Hindu*, 9 November 2019.

5. PTI, 'Citizenship Amendment Act comes into effect from January 10', *India Today*,

10 January 2020. This led to nationwide protests from December 2019, which continued until the first COVID-19 nationwide lockdown in March 2020. See Vasudha Venugopal, 'Delhi lockdown: Anti-CAA protesters removed from Shaheen Bagh, other places', *Economic Times*, 25 March 2020.

6. Shaswati Das, 'NRC will be rolled out across the country before 2024 polls: Amit Shah', *Livemint.com*, 3 December 2019, https://www.livemint.com/news/india/nationwide-nrc-to-be-implemented-before-2024-lok-sabha-polls-amit-shah-11575290024624.html.

7. 'BJP manifesto 2019: Top 10 promises for next 5 years', *India Today*, 8 April 2019.

8. Interviews with various sector and district-level pracharaks of UP, 19 August 2019.

9. PTI, 21 September 2015.

10. *Economic Times*, 22 May 2019.

11. *ABP News*, 14 May 2018.

12. Vikas Pathak, 'National Commission for Backward Classes will get more powers', *The Hindu*, 5 August 2018, and PTI, 6 August 2018.

13. Purnima S. Tripathi, 'A New Calculation in Uttar Pradesh', *Frontline*, Vol. 18, Issue 19, 15–28 September 2001.

14. Ibid.

15. Badri Narayan, *Fractured Tales: Invisibles in Indian Democracy*, New Delhi: Oxford University Press, 2016.

16. Umesh Raghuvanshi, 'Social justice panel submits report, all eyes on Yogi govt's next move', *Hindustan Times*, 1 November 2018.

17. PTI, 10 February 2019.

18. Badri Narayan, 'This is why Yogi govt's "quota within quota" system will be a win-win move in Uttar Pradesh', *ThePrint.com*, 23 August 2019.

19. PTI, 10 February 2019.

20. PM's welcome speech on election of Shri Om Birla as Speaker of Lok Sabha, 19 June 2019.

21. Anil Padmanabhan, 'Social capital in new India key to $5-tn economy', *Livemint.com*, 21 July 2019.

22. Sunil Ambekar, *The RSS: Roadmaps for the 21st Century* (New Delhi: Rupa Publications, 2019).

23. *Business Insider*, 26 May 2019, https://www.businessinsider.in/full-text-of-modi-speech-lok-sabha-election-2019/articleshow/69467611.cms.

24. D.K. Singh, 'Five elements make up Modi's charisma. 4 are beginning to lose lustre', *ThePrint.com*, 27 July 2020.

25. Interview of Kabirpanthi Mahantji, village Shahabpur, Prayagraj, 10 May 2016.
26. Smaller things that make everyday life easy, like providing cooking gas as under the Pradhan Mantri Ujjwala Yojna, or providing scholarships, and so on.

Conclusion

1. 'A five-judge Bench of the Supreme Court on Thursday [in *The State of Punjab & Ors vs Davinder Singh & Ors*] held that States can sub-classify Scheduled Castes and Scheduled Tribes in the Central List to provide preferential treatment to the "weakest out of the weak". The Constitution Bench led by Justice Arun Mishra said reservation has created inequalities within the reserved castes itself.' See Krishnadas Rajagopal, 'States can have sub-groups among SCs/STs: Supreme Court', *The Hindu*, 27 August 2020.
2. 'Realising that the Supreme Court order "diluting" the SC/ST (Prevention of Atrocities) Act was turning out to be a political hot potato, the Narendra Modi Cabinet has decided to bring an amendment bill, which,

if passed by Parliament, will turn the clock back to the original law that had provisions for an FIR without any preliminary enquiry and immediate arrest of a person.' See Rakesh Mohan Chaturvedi, 'Cabinet approves bill to overturn Supreme Court order on SC/ST Act', *Economic Times*, 2 August 2018.

Epilogue

1. Data on Migration, in 2011 Census Data, Office of the Registrar General and Census Commissioner, India, Ministry of Home Affairs, Government of India, https://censusindia.gov.in/2011census/population_enumeration.html; and Samarth Bansal, '45.36 crore Indians are internal migrants', *The Hindu*, 2 December 2016.

2. M.N. Srinivas, *Religion and Society among the Coorgs of South India* (Oxford: Clarendon Press, 1952); and M.N. Srinivas, *Social Change in Modern India* (New Delhi: Sage Publications, 1967).

3. 'Primordial identities' are those that are embedded in age-old experiences. Sukhadeo Thorat and K.S. Newman, *Blocked by Caste: Economic Discrimination in Modern India* (New Delhi: Oxford University Press, 2010, p. 4.

4. For a different translation, see Patrick Olivelle, trans. and ed., 'The Story of Usasti', in *The Early Upanishads: Annotated Text and Translation*, Chapter 2.10 (New York: Oxford University Press, 1998).

5. 'The enemy is not outside, it is within us.' In Georgio Agamben, 'Clarifications', trans. Adam Kotsko, 17 March 2020, translated from the Italian and published at https://itself.blog/2020/03/17/giorgio-agamben-clarifications/.

6. Interview of Shila, 29 May 2020

7. Interview of Devidin, 29 May 2020.

8. Interview of Ramjas, 26 May 2020.

9. Interview of Bipin Dwiwedi, 30 May 2020.

10. Interview of Nagendra, 26 May 2020.

11. Interview of Ram Pratap Chourasia, 27 May 2020 by Brajendra Gautam.

12. Interview of Dhananjay Dixit 25 May by Ram Babu.

13. Field Diary, Ram Babu, Date, 7 June 2020.

14. Field Diary, Ram Babu, 2020.

15. Liz Mathew, 'BJP chief Nadda cautions party leaders: Don't give coronavirus a communal twist', *Indian Express*, 4 April 2020.

SELECT BIBLIOGRAPHY
AND FURTHER READING

Ambekar, S. *The RSS: Roadmaps for the 21st century*. New Delhi: Rupa, 2019.

Andersen, W.K., and Damle, S.K. *The RSS: A View to the Inside*. Gurgaon: Penguin Random House India, 2018.

————. *The Brotherhood in Saffron: The Rashtriya Swayamsevak Sangh and Hindu Revivalism*. Gurgaon: Penguin Random House India, 2019.

Bhattacharjee, Malini. *Disaster Relief and the RSS, Resurrecting 'Religion' through Humanitarianism*. New Delhi: Sage, 2019.

Gopal, K., and Shri Prakash. *Rashtra-Purush Baba Saheb Dr. Bhimrao Ambedkar*. New Delhi: Suruchi Prakashan, 2014.

Goyal, D.R. *Rashtriya Swayamsewak Sangh*. Radhakrishna Prakashan, 1979.

Jha, D.K. *Shadow Armies: Fringe Organizations and Foot Soldiers of Hindutva*. New Delhi: Juggernaut Books, 2017.

Marx, Karl. *Critique of Hegel's 'Philosophy of Right'.* Ed. Joseph O'Malley, trans. Annette Jolin and Joseph O'Malley. New York: Cambridge University Press, 1970; first published 1844.

Narayan, Badri. *Fascinating Hindutva: Saffron Politics and Dalit Mobilisation,* New Delhi: Sage Publications, 2009.

————. *Women Heroes and Dalit Assertion in North India.* In *Cultural Subordination and the Dalit Challenge,* Vol. 5) Sage, New Delhi

Rai, V.N. *Combating Communal Conflicts.* Allahabad: Anamika Prakashan, 1998.

Thorat, S., and Newman, K.S. *Blocked by Caste: Economic Discrimination in Modern India.* New Delhi: Oxford University Press, 2010.

Tripathi, P. 'A New Calculation in Uttar Pradesh'. In *Frontline,* Vol. 18, Issue 19, 15–28 September 2001.

INDEX

Index

Index